When Is Transition Over?

Annette N. Brown
Editor

1999

W.E. Upjohn Institute for Employment Research
Kalamazoo, Michigan

Library of Congress Cataloging-in-Publication Data

When is transition over? / Annette N. Brown, editor.
p. cm.
Essays based on six presentations given at the 33rd Annual Lecture-Seminar Series of the Dept. of Economics at Western Michigan University, held during the 1997–1998 academic year. The lecture series is cosponsored by the Department and the W.E. Upjohn Institute for Employment Research.
Includes bibliographical references (p.) and index.
ISBN 0–88099–196–8 (cloth : alk. paper). — ISBN 0–88099–195–X (paper : alk. paper)
1. Post-communism—Europe, Eastern—Congresses. 2. Capitalism—Europe, Eastern—Congresses. 3. Post-communism—Economic aspects—Europe, Eastern—Congresses. 4. Mixed economy—China—Congresses. 5. China—Economic conditions—1976—Congresses. 6. China—Economic policy—1976—Congresses. 7. China—Politics and government—1976—Congresses. I. Brown, Annette N., 1966– II. Western Michigan University. Dept. of Economics. III. W.E. Upjohn Institute for Employment Research.
HC244.W475 1999
330.12'2'0947—dc21 99–24188
CIP

300 S. Westnedge Avenue
Kalamazoo, Michigan 49007–4686

Cover photo: Border guard posing with tourist at the Berlin Wall.
© Corbis/Owen Franken
Cover design by J. R. Underhill.
Index prepared by Nancy Humphreys.
Printed in the United States of America.

CONTENTS

Introduction 1
Annette N. Brown
Western Michigan University

1 What Is Still Missing? 13
Marie Lavigne
Institut de Sciences Mathématiques et Economiques Appliquées (Paris) and *University of Pau*

2 The End of Transition? 39
Alan Gelb
The World Bank

3 The End of Rent-Seeking 51
Anders Åslund
Carnegie Endowment for International Peace

4 China's Unfinished Economic Transition 69
Nicholas R. Lardy
The Brookings Institution

5 The Transition Is Not Over, but Note the Merits of the Central European Model 77
Jan Švejnar
William Davidson Institute and *University of Michigan*

6 Reforming the Welfare State in Postsocialist Economies 99
János Kornai
Harvard University and *Collegium Budapest*

The Authors 115

Author Index 119

Subject Index 121

Introduction

Annette N. Brown
Western Michigan University

The countries that are changing from communist to postcommunist societies[1] are undergoing a process that has been and continues to be difficult, tumultuous, and often painful for their citizens. In a few short years, people in these countries have lived through more social, political, and economic change than those in more developed, Western economies will see in a lifetime. Both for those living through this process and for those who study and analyze it, there is a recurring question: When is this transition over?

During the 1997–1998 academic year, six distinguished economics scholars—Marie Lavigne, Alan Gelb, Anders Åslund, Nicholas Lardy, Jan Švejnar, and János Kornai—visited Western Michigan University and offered their answers to this question. This book presents their lectures. Their answers are in some ways very different and in others very similar, but always interesting and insightful. In this introduction, I will introduce the speakers, their lectures, and their answers.

THE SPEAKERS

As Marie Lavigne correctly points out in her lecture, the determination of when transition is over will clearly be shaped by the biases of those who are judging, and so it is important to know who those judges are.[2] The participating speakers vary along several meaningful axes. First, they come from different nations: Western and non-Western, transition and nontransition. Lavigne and Åslund are French and Swedish, respectively, giving them a Western European, and possibly even a European Union (EU), perspective. Švejnar and Kornai both grew up under communism in Central Europe, Švejnar in Czechoslovakia and Kornai in Hungary. However, the courses of their adult lives have differed. Švejnar left Czechoslovakia as a young adult and has spent his professional years in the United States as a U.S. citizen, while Kornai struggled for many years as an independent-minded economist in Hungary. In fact, because of his views, Kornai was not allowed to teach in communist Hungary. In a way, their paths have now converged, as both currently split their time between the United States and their home countries, actively contributing to the academy in both. Gelb, as a South African, provides us with a truly outsider's perspective, and Lardy is an American.

Another axis along which the speakers differ is the role they play in the transition process. Lavigne, Lardy, and Kornai are primarily academics, offering their ideas and suggestions principally through the channels of teaching, speaking, and especially writing. Their work then serves as a foundation for policy discussion and initiatives. Gelb, as a World Bank official, has a more direct role. His work requires him not only to study economies but also to recommend specific policies for underpinning the conditions of World Bank loans. He served as the World Bank's Chief Research Economist for transition economies for several years, culminating in his role as Staff Director for the *World Development Report,* devoted exclusively to the issues of transition. Åslund and Švejnar, although both academics, play the most direct roles, as they serve as advisors to transition governments. Åslund was an economic advisor to the Russian government from 1991 to 1994 and currently advises the Ukrainian government. Švejnar was one of the chief architects of the Czech Republic's economic reforms, and he continues to serve as an advisor to Czech President Václav Havel.

A final axis along which the speakers differ is the length of time they have studied communist and postcommunist countries, and thus the breadth of their focus. Lavigne and Kornai have been examining these economies for decades, making them experts not only on economic transition but also on the Soviet-type economies that preceded transition. They have researched and analyzed in detail what we now call "initial conditions." Gelb, Åslund, and Švejnar started their paths to transition economics more recently. In the 1980s, both Gelb and Švejnar wrote about labor management; Åslund wrote his dissertation in the early 1980s about Poland and the former East Germany. Starting in 1989, all three focused sharply on transition. Gelb, during his tenure at the World Bank, has visited, researched, and advised innumerable countries all over the world—in Africa, Asia, Europe, and Central and South America. His points of comparison are not just "East and West," but all points on the globe and many types of economies. Lardy, who concentrates on Chinese reforms, has studied China since the 1970s.

Considered together, these three axes form an "experience space" in which each scholar occupies a distinct point. I leave it to the reader to determine whether and in what ways these experiences affect the views presented in their lectures.

THE LECTURES

The lectures are presented in chronological order, a sequence that also turns out to work well expositionally. Lavigne provides an effective overview of what transition entails, making her analysis an appropriate point of departure, especially for readers less familiar with transition. Gelb goes on to discuss in more detail what has actually occurred during transition and why it occurred that way. Åslund then narrows the focus, emphasizing one of transition's most serious problems, rent-seeking, and its solution. Lardy focuses specifically on China, arguing that the gradualist reforms implemented there are unsustainable. Švejnar picks up the question raised earlier by Lavigne: What is still missing? He presents an extensive list of the transition tasks ahead. Kornai completes the collection by moving beyond transition and discussing what he considers to be post-transition policy.

Lavigne begins by outlining the many legacies of the past and explaining how they negatively affect the transition process. She argues that one significant legacy is the large set of specific social values, which, crediting Kornai, she calls "paternalism"; this legacy means that changes in very basic attitudes are needed before people behave as proper economic "agents." She then describes the basic elements of the transition package, discusses generally how these elements have been implemented, and compares the outcomes. In short, liberalization has been fast (in most cases); stabilization is still fragile; and structural transformation has been slow. Unlike the other authors, she also assesses the outcomes using the Human Development Index, which so far shows improvement only in a few countries. Lavigne lists several barriers to achieving standard market economies and then discusses more specifically the obstacles that the candidate countries face in achieving EU membership. In terms of barriers, she again stresses the problem of attitudes and emphasizes the need to build strong civil societies. For EU membership, the obstacles arise from poorly defined membership conditions that are in some cases stricter than those for current members.

Gelb starts his lecture by elaborating a point that general economic analysis often forgets or ignores, but that the process of economic transition brings to the fore: "Like automobiles, market economies come in many different models." Gelb goes on to make several interesting and compelling arguments. To be successful, reform policies need to be broad-based, as they are highly interdependent, and they need to be sustained, as the cumulative exposure to reforms is more important than the immediate situation in determining the outcomes. Three different forces drive reforms, which naturally lead to differences in the pace and phasing in of change across countries. There are many, if not too many, explanations for transition outcomes. Gelb asks and answers the fascinating question, "Could an alternative policy have worked in Central and Eastern Europe and the former Soviet Union?" In his conclusion, he raises an even more important question, "What kinds of economies and societies will the transition countries turn out to be?" He identifies, in particular, the increasingly unequal distribution of property and income as a major challenge for the future.

Where Gelb gives many explanations for the differences in outcomes among countries, Åslund focuses on one: rent-seeking. He draws a clear line between rent-seeking (which he defines as the extraction of monetary benefits from the government) and inflation and between inflation and gross domestic product performance. He then identifies the various types of rent-seeking and who has benefited the most from this behavior. In explaining why rent-seeking was so much larger in the former Soviet Union than in East-Central Europe, Åslund explores the political-philosophical legacies of the communist system, including the strength of the old communist elite (Nomenklatura); the weaknesses of the postcommunist state, democracy, and civil society; the quality and independence of the media; and the people's understanding of and attitudes toward the market. There were also economic legacies influencing rent-seeking: kleptocracy, perverse relative prices, deep financial crises, and natural resource endowments. Åslund then argues that rent-seeking has been significantly reduced in most of these countries of the former Soviet Union and emphasizes that privatization has served to diminish rather than to increase rent-seeking.

Lardy's lecture is distinct from the others in that it focuses on one country and that the country in question, China, has followed a very different—gradualist—reform path, starting in the 1970s. Lardy compares China's reforms to those of Eastern Europe and the former Soviet Union and argues that in spite of China's superior economic performance, its reforms are unsustainable. Three issues raise particular concern: enterprise performance and debt, nonperforming bank loans, and declining tax revenues. In the second part of the lecture, Lardy examines the necessary reform of China's banking sector in more detail. It would be extremely difficult for China to default on household liabilities as Russia did, because the volume of household savings is tremendous. It would also be infeasible for China to gradually recapitalize banks through reinvestment of profits as Hungary did, because the necessary recapitalization is too great. Instead, Lardy recommends that China recapitalize by injecting government bonds into these banks.

Švejnar, in the first half of his lecture, describes the "Central European model" of transition and compares and contrasts it with two other models, the "Asian model" and the "Russian and NIS model."[3] He identifies several key areas where the transition outcomes have been systematic, or similar, across the Central European countries, chief among them being that all of these countries now have functioning market economies. More interesting, perhaps, are the distinctive results that he identifies among these countries, which so often are considered as a group. Privatization has proceeded unevenly; labor force adjustment has differed significantly; and various exchange rate policies have resulted in diverse foreign trade performances. The second half of the lecture focuses on the challenges ahead for Central Europe. Although other speakers visit this theme, Švejnar provides the most detail, giving what Lavigne might call a full prescription for finishing transition in Central Europe. The foremost challenge, Švejnar argues, is to generate and sustain high rates of growth. The building blocks for this growth include such strategies as high rates of efficiently placed investment, human capital development, and establishing effective corporate governance.

Kornai sets out to discuss transformation rather than transition, where transformation comprises the processes following transition that improve the functioning of a capitalist system. An important part of transformation, not just in formerly communist countries but also in some Western countries, is the reform of the welfare state. Kornai begins his discussion of these reforms by stating explicitly the ethical principles underlying his analysis: respect for individual sovereignty, moral obligation to solidarity, and commitment to democracy and the transparency of public decision-making processes. The initial conditions in any transforming economy determine which of these principles might be problematic. Kornai argues that there is a clear need for health care reform in Hungary. Hungarians are currently demanding improvements in the quality of their health care system without understanding who pays for this service. He offers several concrete suggestions as to how the provision of health care can be changed in line with his underlying ethical principles.

The lectures share several threads. All of the speakers, even Kornai implicitly, divide the transition economies into three groups: Central and Eastern Europe (CEE), where Central Europe (Poland, the Czech Republic, Slovakia, and Hungary) receives more attention than Eastern Europe; the former Soviet Union, where Russia and Ukraine are emphasized and the Baltics are often considered to be exceptions; and China and Vietnam, which, if for no other reason, are different because they are still communist. All of the speakers account for the initial conditions, or legacies, in their analysis. In particular, they all mention the need to change people's attitudes towards and understanding of capitalism and market economies. Related to these changes at the individual level, most also mention the necessity to develop strong civil societies, in which institutions support both capitalism and democracy. The speakers generally consider transition in two stages: the first primarily involves liberalization and stabilization, and the second encompasses a myriad of structural reforms. They roughly agree that the first stage is complete in many of the countries, but that progress and success in the second stage have been quite mixed. Finally, most emphasize the concept of transparency as an important goal in a variety of contexts. The lectures also differ in many ways, and perhaps the most interesting divergence lies in the answers that are presented.

THE ANSWERS

When is transition over? Lavigne responds directly, "I think the question is unanswerable." Indirectly, however, she offers another reply: transition is over for the CEE countries when they become members of the EU. This answer is important to consider because it is obvious to many people in Europe, but Lavigne deems it unworkable because the EU conditions are vague and unequally applied. Although she does not offer her own criteria for the end of transition, Lavigne does conclude that it is not over yet. Gelb answers the question straightaway: "Transition is over when the problems and the policy issues confronted by today's 'transition countries' resemble those faced by other countries at similar levels of development." He further states that no matter how this definition is operationalized, the "transition countries are not there yet."

Åslund measures the end of transition according to the reduction of rent-seeking, which reflects a variety of institutional reforms. According to his standard, Åslund concludes that transition is over in all but a few countries. Lardy argues that transition in China will not be complete until three sectors are aggressively reformed: state-owned enterprises, the financial sector, and government service provision. Švejnar presents two conditions for transition to be over: central planning is abolished, and an efficiently functioning market system takes its place. According to these conditions, he concludes that transition is not over in any of the considered economies. Kornai answers with the most precision. Transition is over when three, and only three, criteria are met: the communist party no longer has monopoly power; the dominant part of the means of production is privately owned; and the market is the dominant coordinator of economic activities. Using these criteria, he concludes that transition in Hungary is over, and probably would conclude that it is over in several other countries as well.

We can group these answers into three categories. Kornai's answer is systemic; that is, he looks at changes in the features of the economic systems to judge when transition is over. He makes clear that the new system, the endpoint of transition, is a market economy as defined by his specific criteria. Gelb's answer also contains a strong systemic component but is more obscure than Kornai's. Gelb defends this obscurity by arguing that models of market economies vary greatly. Each transition economy will have its own terminus of transition, which may or may not resemble a Western market economy. Therefore, the indication seems to be when the economy resembles some kind of market system rather than still being distinguished by its communist legacy. In spite of a similarity in their criteria, Kornai and Gelb reach very different conclusions. Kornai believes that transition is over, at least in some countries, while Gelb says none of the countries has reached this stage.

In the second category, the answers are based on outcomes. Lavigne considers and then discards the criterion that countries gain EU membership. While such a result is certainly dependent on systemic changes, the suggested criterion itself examines just the outcomes. Švejnar also proposes a results-based answer: the end of transition is the state of an advanced market economy. Again, a systemic component is involved, especially in the first condition of eliminating central planning, but the ultimate condition is based on outcomes. Švejnar defines efficient functioning to include achieving rapid and sustainable rates of growth and becoming compatible with advanced market economies. In short, these answers suggest that transition is over not just when economies operate differently, but also when they operate successfully. As a result, although Švejnar and Kornai clearly agree that the countries of Central Europe are market economies, Švejnar says they have at least 10 years to go, while Kornai says transition is over.

Åslund's and Lardy's answers, which I will call "institutional," fall somewhere in the middle. Although the rent-seeking that Åslund examines arises from the systemic changes, clearly the new market system is considered to be part of his endpoint. For example, the liberalizations of domestic prices and trade represent two measures toward eliminating rent-seeking that are also part of the systemic change. However, Åslund's endpoint encompasses more. Policies to abolish rent-seeking include the liberalization of foreign trade, the unification of the exchange rate, and the elimination of interest subsidies. He also indicates that a strong central bank is important. With these latter conditions, Åslund includes elements of institutional, or structural, change in his criteria for the end of transition.

Like Åslund, Lardy identifies specific institutional reforms, beyond the systemic changes, that are required for the completion of transition in China. State-owned enterprises need to be restructured so that they are forced to be profitable and desist from accumulating large bank debts. The financial sector, the emphasis of the lecture, needs to be recapitalized and reformed so that banks operate as effective financial intermediaries. The government needs to change its operation as well. It needs to collect more tax revenues and increase its role as a provider of social services so that the enterprises can focus on their primary production. These criteria are clearly institutional, especially since Lardy avoids calling for the privatization of state-owned enterprises, which would be a more systemic change.

Gelb also highlights institutional determinants. For example, he suggests that, even with private ownership (a systemic feature), the Czech voucher funds (an institutional element) will make the Czech economy distinctive, and thus in transition, for some time to come. He concludes that, in practice, the core systemic changes and the combination of institutional changes go hand-in-hand in moving an economy toward its transition endpoint. Compared with Åslund's and Lardy's approaches, however, Gelb's is again more obscure. Where for Åslund rent-seeking identifies a fairly specific set of necessary institutions, Gelb allows that the combinations will vary according to different levels of development.

In sum, the answers are very different, and the old maxim that economists never agree seems to hold true. The question is academic, however, and more important than the proclamation about whether or not transition is over is the analysis of the problems these countries still face and the recommendations for what can and should be done to address them. Along these lines, the speakers tend to agree.

POSTSCRIPT

In more than a year of organizing and implementing this lecture series, and during many discussions with the participating scholars, with my students in the accompanying courses, and with my colleagues in the field, I have often pondered the end-of-transition question. As Kornai says, each of us who works on transition has his or her own criteria, and I offer mine as an additional point of comparison.

Transition is over when the organization of production reaches a long-run, market equilibrium. Gelb actually provides examples for this criterion when he argues that transition will not be over in countries such as Romania and Armenia, which privatized agricultural land into very small parcels, until market forces bring about the consolidation of land into commercial farms; similarly, transition will not be over in Russia until landholding shifts away from large joint-stock company farms. In general, there are many features of these countries' productive structures that are inherited from the communist period, such as too much military production and not enough consumer goods production, or that are created by the transition process, as in the small privatized landholdings in Romania and Armenia, that are not in long-run equilibrium in the market economy. While these features continue to exist, the economies are, by definition really, still in transition.

Clearly, the productive structure of any market economy is constantly evolving, and these changes on the margin are vital for the continued success of the system. I do not mean to say that transition is over when the organization of production stops changing. But rather, transition is over when productive structure has been transformed from its inherited organization to a structure that continues to change only slowly with the evolution of the economy. For example, when the processes of entry, exit, expansion, and contraction act to completely reshape industries, the economy is still in transition. When these processes settle such that they only change overall industry structure during a long period of time, then transition is over. Like Gelb's, my endpoints are obscure, because we do not know *a priori* what the long-run equilibria will resemble. We do not even know whether for any given country there is one, or more than one, possible equilibrium. Thus, this answer, like many answers to academic questions, leads to more questions.

NOTES

NOTE: My comments here benefited from discussion in two minicourses I taught in conjunction with this lecture series, and I would like to thank the students in those courses: Kyung Suk Cho, Jason Courtney, Jason Craig, Erin Dunleavy, Wai Kong Foong, Hans Gottschaldt, Robert Jacox, Wendelin Knobloch, Kyle Krawiec, Ali Mirmiran, and Christopher Polk. I would also like to thank J. David Brown for comments on this chapter.

1. In a few cases, such as China, these may be countries that are simply moving to more market-oriented economies.
2. Short biographies are presented at the end of this book.
3. NIS = Newly Independent States (of the former Soviet Union).

1 What Is Still Missing?

Marie Lavigne
Institut de Sciences Mathématiques et Economiques Appliquées (Paris)
and *University of Pau*

One may liken the situation of any country in transition to the case of a man who has been severely ill for years. Nobody really thought that his condition would improve. All of a sudden, there is a miracle: a new medicine is discovered. The patient's doctor decides to apply this new approach—a shock therapy—not quite knowing what is going to come of it. Then the miracle goes on: the patient is on his feet again, following a terrible fever. Several years pass. Slowly the patient regains his former functions. There are moments of despair. The process is not even. Sometimes there are bouts of fever. Sometimes the patient has the impression that he is worse than before; for months, his performance declines. Not that he regrets the treatment; the hope is there, and he would not want to return to his previous condition. Sometimes he is angry at the doctor, who sets him impossible targets; he does not want to undergo all these exercises every day. However, little by little, things are steadying. One day, the patient sees that he has indeed not only regained his previous level, but has gone beyond that.

At this point, his doctor tells him that he no longer needs assistance and that he is a healthy man again. His friends tell him the same, as they are tired of being involved in this recovery process. The patient himself is not so sure about his condition. He does not feel all right. Some days he is limping again. A small fever persists. Many unwanted occurrences bother him: he is not quite able to coordinate all his movements, he does or says things that he does not want to do or say, and he loses his temper too often. A number of other elements are missing as well and prevent him from feeling really good. He cannot find the right clothes, he does not work quite properly, and sometimes his memory is failing.

Nevertheless, he resolves to go to his former club and to request readmission. His old buddies are kind but stern. So much time has elapsed since he had to leave the group. The members are ready to consider his application, but they impose several demanding conditions. He is ready to fulfill these requirements even if again it takes time, because he feels that once he is readmitted, he will be able to say, "Yes, now I am cured, I am a normal person."

You must have recognized the actors and the plot of this short story. The patient is a transition country, the doctor is the International Monetary Fund (IMF), the friends are international organizations or other governments providing assistance, and the European Union (EU), of course, is the club. Inflation is the recurrent fever. You may pinpoint the fall of output or slowdown in growth, the lengthy and uncompleted process of structural transformation, the unwanted phenomena, and the missing elements in the process. At least the Eastern or Central European patient is hopeful about his admission to the club. However, when will a patient who is not considered for the club be cured? That is the question facing Russia and many other countries of the former Soviet Union area.

So, when is transition over? The prime minister of the Czech Republic, Václav Klaus, claimed in December 1995 that transition was finished as far as his country was concerned, and this claim seemed reasonable enough. According to a general view, the transition from plan to market is largely completed in Central Europe, and to a lesser extent in Southeast Europe and in the Baltic countries. It is yet to be completed in the former Soviet Union space. Usually the performance is assessed on the basis of several criteria:

- a successful stabilization-cum-liberalization policy
- a solid launching of structural transformation
- the building up of conditions for sustainable growth
- progress in integration in the world economy, and, particularly, in the European economy

I will outline the transition process with a view to identifying what is still missing: what the patient needs to join the club, and what his neighbor who will not be joining the club needs to become healthy. I will describe transition according to the following features: the legacies of the previous system, the building blocks of the transition package, the outcomes of macroeconomic reform and structural transformation, and finally, what still has to be done so as to complete the transition process. This discussion leads to four conclusions. The legacies of the past are still binding, and the new market economies bear the traces of this history. The initial measures did not encompass the whole process of transition and largely left aside the complex task of building a market environment. The outcomes are mixed; several crises in 1996–1997 showed how fragile transition still is. Much has yet to be done to complete the process.

The countries in transition from a planned to a market economy may be grouped into four broad subsets according to a geopolitical division:

- **Group One** consists of the Central and Eastern European countries, including the four Central European countries (Poland, Hungary, the Czech Republic, Slovakia) plus Slovenia (the core "Visegrad" group); Bulgaria and Romania; and the three Baltic States (Estonia, Latvia, and Lithuania). This group comprises 10 countries that have applied to become members of the EU. Hence, the completion of the transition process is very much linked with these countries' meeting the conditions for becoming members and with the "pre-accession strategy" conducted in coordination with the EU. Albania may be included in this group in the future.
- **Group Two** includes the countries of the Commonwealth of Independent States (CIS), with particular attention to Russia, which has played, and is bound to play, a decisive role in the CIS region and in the patterns of transition there.
- **Group Three** includes the Asian countries in transition, with special attention to China and Vietnam. The other Indochinese countries, Laos and Cambodia, should also be included in this group, as well as Mongolia. This group is very different from the others. China and Vietnam share three main features: their commitment to a communist political regime, economic underdevelopment, and an Asian-type strategy of growth and industrialization in the framework of transition to the market.

- **Group Four** includes the countries that are for the time being largely left out of discussion because of the political context, for example, the countries of the former Yugoslavia (Slovenia excepted).

I shall focus mainly on the two first groups.

THE LEGACIES OF THE PAST

History still heavily constrains the transition process. Contrary to an optimistic view that prevailed at the beginning of transition, it was not enough to overthrow the communist regime in order to clear the way for a smooth and full-fledged operation of the market. My stance is that most of these legacies, if not all, are negative from the point of view of the transition to a new system. This stance does not mean that I regard all of the achievements of the old system as negative. Obviously, the system was very wasteful in human and material resources at the times when it yielded its higher rates of growth. Later, it failed to achieve modernization and left all its countries lagging behind Western, developed economies. It caused great damage to the environment. However, fundamental needs were satisfied, including high standards of collective consumption in health and education. A great degree of security characterized these societies, with protection against unemployment and provision of basic goods and services on a rather egalitarian basis, even taking into account hidden inequalities and a large amount of politically based corruption. I present the legacies roughly according to a scheme devised by János Kornai. There are three types, with examples for each: systemic legacies, functional legacies, and assets and liabilities.

The first systemic legacy is the ideological and political monopoly of the Communist Party. Although standard state institutions existed, there was no state policy outside the party's decision. Hence, once the party's structure collapsed, the state institutions were not prepared to fulfill their functions. One thus had the impression of a "demise of the state" in the operation of the judiciary, the executive branch (ministries), and the state administration. The fact that one could find "institutions" in the planned economies with the same names as in market economies ("banks," "ministries," "agencies") gave the false impression that, once the system had collapsed, these entities could function as market institutions.

Second, the system was characterized by dominant state (collective) ownership of the means of production. The state sector was huge, meaning that privatization is much more difficult than the same process in market economies. Even in those economies that have privatized faster and more extensively than others, there remains a very large residual state sector. In the state-owned enterprises (SOEs) that have been formally privatized, the weight of the "insiders" (the former management, which generally uses the employees to support it) is very big. As the SOEs were large, their privatization may mean a shift from public to private monopolies; thus, de-monopolization is an issue. The SOEs were not only production enterprises, but also social security institutions: they provided for such needs as health care, child care, and housing, so that the building of an independent Western-type social safety net is very difficult.

The third systemic legacy is central planning. As a result, there is now a distrust of all forms of planning, including strategic planning as practiced in Western governments and big corporations. Yet there is a surviving "planning mentality" in managing stabilization; for example, the "targets" set by the IMF have often been treated like plan assignments. The same mentality survives in managing structural transformation; for example, privatization programs are essentially state undertakings tightly controlled by the government.[1] A lack of understanding of market-type coordination, a "legacy" shared by many outside advisers as well,[2] leads to the idea that, as soon as planning is abolished, a market economy immediately begins to operate.

Two of the functional legacies are a distorted production structure and autarky. The production structure was a consequence of the Soviet strategy of extensive growth imposed upon Central and Eastern Europe. That policy left the countries in transition with an overdeveloped heavy industry sector, lacking competitiveness with Western markets. In addition, the ratio of exports to gross domestic product (GDP) was lower than in market economies of similar dimensions, and most of the trade that did take place was concentrated in Council for Mutual Economic Assistance (Comecon) countries. Hence, the demise of Comecon created a substantial shock.

A less concrete but just as important functional legacy is the inheritance of a wide set of specific social values. The relationship between the state and the economic agent was marked by what Kornai calls "paternalism." The state enterprise had to carry on political and social functions, and the individual was protected by the state "from cradle to grave." Many individual legacies follow from paternalism: the belief of the plant managers that they will be bailed out even if their operating costs exceed their revenues (this is the definition of the "soft budget constraint"); the belief of the bank managers that they have to supply "their" client enterprises with credit whenever the latter ask for it; the belief of the workers that they have to be paid just for showing up at the workplace and that they cannot be fired. Even under the conditions of transition, these legacies of an implicit "social" contract and of an implicit "state-enterprise" contract often remain, as in Russia.

Similarly, due to such lingering social values, the image of the "good" manager as someone who has a positive relationship with the authorities and is by principle reluctant to lay off workers remains in the countries that are less advanced in the transition process. By contrast, the efficient manager who tries to reduce costs and increase profits, and who is not adverse to downsizing, has the negative image of a speculator, if not of a mafioso. Entrepreneurial skills as such are not favorably judged.

Human capital and physical infrastructure comprise two legacies that may be seen as assets or as liabilities. The stock of human capital (skilled workforce) is usually viewed as a positive legacy of the system. However, the innovative capacity of individuals was hampered by the obsolescence of techniques and by the very weak link between research and applied development. Hence, the remaining legacy of human capital is more a liability than an asset, and the quality of human capital is rapidly diminishing in the transition process, along with the decline of health and education indicators, which are embodied in the Human Development Index. The physical infrastructure is obsolete and not adapted to the needs of modern market economies, as it was developed out of strategic and military considerations more than out of considerations linked to the development of civilian economies. This infrastructure may be an asset, as in the use of the former military telecommunications network for civilian needs, but generally it is a liability, as in the case of roads.

Why are these legacies detrimental to the course of transition? The answer is because they cannot be separated from the system. For example, quasi-full employment went with low productivity; skills gained in school and professional education went with weak incentives for efficient activity; and low-cost housing led to an overall deterioration of the civilian housing stock.

THE TRANSITION PACKAGE

The building blocks for transition have basically been the same for all of the countries that engaged effectively in reform. The program packages have been devised by experts from the countries in transition (who are often trained in Western economics) and have been supplemented with additional features following agreements with the IMF. The standard package is an adaptation of the "Washington consensus."[3] The package may be divided into three sections:

- initial liberalization of consumer and producer prices, of domestic and foreign trade, and of foreign exchange transactions
- stabilization aimed at resolving macroeconomic imbalances[4]
- beginning of structural transformation

There was much discussion initially about the sequencing and the speed of the reforms. In fact, these debates lost relevance rather quickly, as fine-tuning policies appeared illusory in economies characterized by rather primitive market conditions, and as the choice between the "big bang" (or "shock therapy") model and the "gradualist" model was largely artificial. Stabilization and liberalization had to be conducted fast (otherwise there could be no reform). Transformation had to take time, and what mattered was to announce what would be done and to establish credibility. When one looks at the nations in transition overall, including those in the former Soviet Union, the true dividing line lies between the countries that moved toward reform (which does not exclude traveling in the reverse direction, as in the case of Bulgaria for some years), which also comprise all the applicants to EU membership, and the countries that have hardly begun implementing reform (most of the CIS states) or have implemented it in an erratic way (Russia).

The package of measures to be taken everywhere has encompassed the following steps. First, very soon (if possible, on day one), take early liberalization measures—of prices (with the usual exceptions: housing, utilities, and energy to be freed up to several years later), of domestic trade, and of foreign trade and foreign exchange transactions. Also on day one (in the case of "shock therapy"), begin stabilization measures aimed at curbing inflation, reducing the budget deficit, and steadying the exchange rate. Third, to be announced on day one but to be completed much later, undertake long-term measures of structural transformation, including privatization (first, small-scale privatization and later, large-scale privatization of big firms), banking reform, the introduction of a capital market, tax and social security reform, and establishment of environmental and industrial policies.

The means and instruments of achieving these objectives have depended on the tasks themselves. For liberalization, it was supposed that it would be enough for the authorities just to end state involvement. For stabilization, the standard measures used in market economies were expected to bring about the desired results. Nevertheless, the market had not yet arrived; it was to be effected through structural reform.

Price liberalization, through the emergence of market-clearing prices, led very quickly (almost overnight, in the case of Poland) to the curtailment of shortages. Several outcomes have become evident. All economic agents are now allowed to buy and sell. Street trade has expanded, and private shops have opened. However, the large inherited wholesale (supplier) organizations in most cases have remained for some time. The state retail outlets have sometimes been taken over by foreign distribution chains. State foreign trade organizations have been dismantled, and enterprises may conduct foreign trade transactions on their own. Quantitative restrictions on foreign trade have been abolished, and tariffs have been reduced. Households may sell and buy foreign currency. The prices of foreign currency are unified and either freed (floating-rate regime), or fixed at a very low rate, which may be the previous black-market rate or be determined along various regimes (such as managed float, crawling peg, or crawling bands). In exceptional cases, a currency board has been established (in Estonia, Lithuania, and Bulgaria in 1997). Convertibility for current account transactions has become the rule.

The instruments of stabilization have included restrictive monetary policy and the restoration of positive real interest rates. This strategy is considered to be the orthodox approach, where the interest rate is the main anchor of stabilization policy. Other times, governments have established incomes policy with controls on wage increases and weak indexation of wages on price rises; this is the heterodox approach (Bruno 1992). Taxes have been increased, usually with little effect because of tax evasion and lack of tax reform. Public expenditures have been cut even beyond the reduction of price subsidies. While the domestic currency has been sharply devalued from the outset, stabilization policy should avoid further devaluation (an extreme solution is to adopt a currency board regime) as well as an appreciation of the real exchange rate.

There are many early measures of structural reform, implemented in different order and at diverse speeds by the various countries. Privatization, a major task of transition, has often been undertaken in two stages: the immediate beginning of "small privatization" (selling small public property), and preparing and launching large-scale privatization, which takes several years. One country (the Czech Republic) proceeded quickly to mass privatization on the basis of "voucher" distribution of state-owned assets, and in most countries (except Hungary), mass privatization has been a component of the large privatization strategy.

Financial markets are another major focus of structural transformation. Reform of the banking sector requires the introduction of a two-tier banking system (if it did not exist already), turning the state commercial banks into private banks or incorporating them, changing banking operations, beginning the financial restructuring of banks (through consolidating bad loans or other methods), and implementing bankruptcy laws. Countries have also set up stock exchanges and developed domestic securities (often in relation to privatization).

Finally, there are several measures involved in the structural reformation of the state. Governments have begun to create modern tax regimes, generalize income taxes, set up a value-added tax, and improve tax collection. They must also replace what was an all-embracing social security system basically managed by the SOEs with a modern system combining state allowances and private insurance schemes. The reform here is very difficult because of lack of means and of institutions and because strong political and social opposition usually exists (Lavigne 1995).

THE OUTCOMES

The outcomes of transition thus far should be assessed by looking at real and at monetary-financial economic indicators, which are presented in Tables 1, 2, and 3. There are many similarities among the countries. There has been a global deterioration in the "human development" situation, as measured by the set of criteria used by the United Nations Development Program (UNDP) (Table 1, p. 30). The Human Development Index improved only in Poland. There was a large drop in output for all the transition countries in the 1990s (Table 2), followed by recoveries of varying strengths in Central and Eastern Europe, but not yet in the former Soviet Union. There was a still deeper drop in investment in most cases, with a protracted recovery. Unemployment rates in Central and Eastern Europe have stabilized at relatively high levels (with the exception of the Czech Republic) as compared with Western European rates. Real incomes fell, followed by a modest increase, especially when incomes are measured in dollars, which points to an appreciation of the real interest rate.

Most countries had similar outbursts of inflation, followed by a stabilization of the inflation rate at moderate to high levels. Even in the most successful countries, the inflation rate is still well above the Western European average. Many have had great difficulties in maintaining budgetary deficits at "acceptable" levels (as defined in IMF packages), although some have succeeded, such as the Czech Republic, Slovakia, and Slovenia. Exchange rate stabilization has been successful, with exceptions. However, there has been sharp deterioration of foreign trade and current account balances and emerging problems with short-term capital inflows (Table 3).

Structural transformation in terms of the management and governance of enterprises has lagged, even though privatization is supposed to have been largely achieved. Banking and financial reforms and the modernization of social security systems have also been slow.

The bottom line is that recovery, even when underway, is impaired by factors on the supply side, such as the impact of the initial cuts in investment, and by both domestic and foreign factors on the demand side. Also, macroeconomic stabilization is still fragile. The question to be asked is whether the strategies themselves explain these results, or if they are due to the quality of the implementation, or to the initial situation of each country. A debated topic is the link between liberalization, on the one hand, and growth and inflation, on the other hand. The World Bank *World Development Report 1996*, devoted to the countries in transition, raised the issue, which has been elaborated upon in de Melo and Gelb (1996) and in Fisher, Sahay, and Vegh (1997). The conclusion is that growth and the control of inflation go together and that both are positively related to liberalization. This analysis leaves aside the slow progress in structural reform, which itself may affect growth and stabilization. The slackening of growth in 1996 and the wave of crises in 1996–1997 that hit not only "lagging reformers" such as Albania, Bulgaria, and Romania, but also the Czech Republic, exemplify this impact.

THE NEW MARKET ECONOMIES IN TRANSITION COUNTRIES

What remains to be done to complete the transition process? For the countries that have applied for membership in the EU, the most immediate objective is to meet the conditions imposed by the EU. Does this mean that once the conditions are met (and the countries are accepted in the EU, with a new "transition" period ahead), the systemic transition is over? First, the EU conditions do not address the question of a sustainable growth strategy. Second, the accession here deals with countries that have not yet created a market economy in the Western sense. In the case of the countries belonging to the former Soviet Union, the prospects are still more remote. Table 4 offers an assessment of the structural achievements of a sample of countries. Before considering the EU conditions further, I will list several frequently mentioned obstacles still faced in the building of standard market economies.

An obstacle on which many observers focus, especially in the case of Russia, is the development of organized crime and corruption on an unusually high level. The combination of the experience of the clandestine mafias of the past and the high technology and financial means available to the modern Western criminal groups, which have quickly established links with the ex-Soviet and Eastern European mafias, can be extremely detrimental. Related to the development of economic crime, an egalitarian society has been replaced by an unequal society (see the evolution of the Gini coefficients in Table 1) with an uneven distribution of income and wealth. Such a pattern is not uncommon in developing nations, but the countries in transition offer a wide variety of "niches" to exploit in the black and gray economic sectors, allowing quick and large gains (for example, the "give-away" forms of privatization, the opportunities of the emergent capital markets, and the use of domestic or foreign trade networks). These niches mean that large and influential circles of economic actors are opposed to the establishment of a transparent market economy.

Efficient market institutions are still lacking, such as working bankruptcy procedures, clear corporate governance rules, prudential rules for the banking system, regulation of the capital markets, effective tax collection, and a flexible labor market. Also needed is efficient state administration, which would be able to implement laws without discrimination and without excessive red tape in order to ensure adequate protection for investors (foreign and domestic) and for partners in business contracts, consumers, and other economic agents. A new, positive vision of the character of the state (neither totalitarian nor paternalistic) is required, instead of an excessive confidence in the market mechanism. The *World Development Report 1997*, devoted to the role of the state in a market economy, discusses what should be done in transition countries, as well as in other developing countries (World Bank 1997b, pp. 164–165).

Next in this list of obstacles is the lack of appropriate social policies. In the countries in transition, one has witnessed a deterioration in the situation of pensioners, who are often below the poverty line, and, at the same time, a growing strain on the budget due to the increasing number of pensioners. This is especially true as the new regimes have usually kept the rather generous age conditions for being eligible for a pension. Less and less are health and education services provided free of charge, especially at high-quality levels (e.g., specialized medical care, university and professional education), while standard services are quickly deteriorating.

More generally speaking, these countries—even those that seem the most mature and ready to integrate in the European economy as members of the EU—do not yet display sound relations between the state and civil society. Despite privatization and the reduction in government social expenditures, people still count on the state for their well-being or at least for the alleviation of their hardships, and rightly so: in some instances, the authorities still behave as did the old "paternalistic" state, especially when this behavior does not entail direct budgetary expenditures. A good case is the low level of unemployment in the Czech Republic. Did the government willingly sustain employment? It could not be so, especially when, at the same time, the authorities complained about low productivity in the state-owned sector. However, bankruptcy proceedings were not initiated against insolvent enterprises, and declining industries were still supported by the state, often on the grounds that they provided exports. In addition, managers in the state-owned sector often considered their first task to be the preservation of employment.

In turn, the survival of past attitudes toward the state has many consequences. One is the vulnerability of the people to populist pledges from leaders or would-be leaders. Candidates in elections are readily believed when they promise their constituencies "catching up" in terms of welfare or in the improvement of their living standards. What makes it easy is the existence of ready-made scapegoats such as the IMF or the EU. Another consequence of old attitudes is the weakness of societal organizations, because people are used to turning to the state, which previously was tantamount to the party. There were no responsible trade unions able to negotiate with employers and representatives of the government, and no consumer and other associations and foundations. Where these institutions have appeared, they are only beginning to get adjusted to their new functions.

We may thus conclude that, for some time, these new market economies will be mixed economies in two senses. First, they will remain strongly influenced by state policies, both as a residual of the past (even if it is not acknowledged by their governments) and as a necessity in the context of institution-building and growth-promoting action. Second, they will lag behind the advanced market economies in development levels and in fullness of markets, and even behind the most successful emergent economies of Asia or Latin America in the context of a global economy.

The outside world can and does contribute (in terms of assistance, foreign investment, and access to markets). However, this help, be it multilateral or bilateral, public or private, is always dictated by the general interests of the donors, investors, or partners. Multilateral assistance is never so considerable as when the issue invokes a global crisis (Mexico in 1994, Thailand in 1997). The initial aim of foreign investment is not the promoting of structural transformation and managerial skills: investors want profits and markets first. This means that the recipient countries must themselves absorb assistance and investments efficiently, and such an absorption is not automatically generated by the market.

Do the EU conditions for membership imposed on the Central and Eastern European countries constitute useful criteria that enable us to say, once they are met, that transition is over? It is likely that they do not. In fact, the implementation of these conditions may be hindered by problems with definitions, and, in many cases, these stipulations are stricter than those placed on current member countries.

One condition of the EU pre-accession strategy (first defined in the "Copenhagen Principles" stated in 1993) is that the country must be a stable, pluralist democracy committed to the rule of law, respect for human rights, and protection of minorities. Many transition countries do still have problems in these areas, including discrimination against minorities, lack of freedom of the press, and corruption in judiciary systems. These requirements, however, were not imposed on previous candidates to the EU. Clearly, issues such as freedom of the press are more obvious in the formerly communist countries, but the Western European countries are certainly not immune to problems of corruption and discrimination.

A second condition of the strategy is that the candidate be an established market economy. What is "an established market economy"? No explanation is given, and the implication seems to be that you know a market economy when you see one. Many will consider the Central and Eastern European countries to be established market economies only when they become EU members: the condition is the outcome.

A third condition is that the economy be able to cope with competitive forces and market pressures within the EU. Again, no explanation is provided. The stipulation implies that the economy be truly liberalized and not protectionist, that it abstain from subsidizing firms or sectors, and that current account deficits be covered by inflows of long-term capital foreign direct investment (FDI) rather than by growing short-term indebtedness. A fourth condition is that the applicant be able to assume the obligations of membership, in particular as far as the *acquis communautaire* is concerned.[5] These obligations include an enormous number of detailed requirements, which continue to evolve over time. The extent of compliance with all of them is largely a matter of political assessment.

An implicit condition of accession is that stabilization must be complete. Stabilization, as we saw above, entails controlling inflation, the ratio of the budget deficit to GDP, and the level of public debt, as well as controlling the current account deficit without resorting to devaluation. However, these conditions are essentially the Maastricht convergence criteria, which were not to be imposed on the applicant countries.

When is transition over? As alluded to by the parable at the beginning of my paper, that determination is clearly shaped by the biases of those who are judging. In sum, I think the question is unanswerable.

NOTES

1. These programs are tightly controlled by the state without any countervailing power from large private corporations, with which Western governments have to cope when they try to control privatization.
2. In the beginning of transition, many advisors entertained the illusion that it was enough to lift the controls and "let the cards fall" to get a fully fledged market. For instance, see Sachs (1993, p. xii): "Markets spring up as soon as central planning bureaucrats vacate the field."
3. See Williamson (1994). The Washington consensus sums up the standard package recommended by the World Bank and the IMF to the developing countries with balance of payments problems in the 1980s.
4. These two building blocks have sometimes been lumped together in a "stabilization-cum-liberalization" concept.

5. In EU parlance, *acquis communautaire* encompasses all the decisions and legal provisions of any kind implemented since the relevant treaties among the members have been ratified, as well as the national laws based on these decisions and provisions.

References

Bruno, Michael. 1992. "Stabilization and Reform in Eastern Europe: A Preliminary Evaluation." *IMF Staff Papers* 39(4): 741–77.

de Melo, Marta, and Alan Gelb. 1996. "A Comparative Analysis of Twenty-Eight Transition Economies in Europe and Asia." *Post-Soviet Geography and Economics* 37(5): 265–285.

EBRD (European Bank for Reconstruction and Development). 1996. *Transition Report*. London.

———. 1997. *Transition Report Update*, April. London.

ECE/UN (Economic Commission for Europe of the United Nations). 1997. *Economic Survey of Europe in 1996–1997*. Geneva and New York.

Fisher, Stanley, Ratna Sahay, and Carlos A. Vegh. 1997. "From Transition to Market: Evidence and Growth Prospects." In *Lessons from Economic Transition: Central and Eastern Europe in the 1990s,* Salvatore Zecchini, ed. Paris: OECD, pp. 79–101.

Lavigne, Marie. 1995. *The Economics of Transition, from Socialist Economy to Market Economy.* London: Macmillan; New York: St Martin's Press.

Podkaminer, Leon, Helen Boss, Rumen Dobrinsky, Vladimir Gligorov, Peter Havlik, Gábor Hunya, Kazimierz Laski, Zdenek Lukas, Josef Pöschl, Sándor Richter, Waltraut Urban, and Hermine Vidovic. 1997. *Year-end 1996: Mixed Results in the Transition Countries.* Vienna: Weiner Institut für Internationale Wirtschaftsvergleiche (WIIW), Research Report no. 233.

Podkaminer, Leon, Helen Boss, Rumen Dobrinsky, Vladimir Gligorov, Peter Havlik, Gábor Hunya, Zdenek Lukas, Josef Pöschl, Sándor Richter, and Hermine Vidovic. 1998. *Transition Countries: 1997 External Deficits Lower Than Feared, Stability Again a Priority.* Vienna: Weiner Institut für Internationale Wirtschaftsvergleiche (WIIW), Research Report no. 243.

Sachs, Jeffrey D. 1993. *Poland's Jump to the Market Economy.* Cambridge: MIT Press.

UNDP (United National Development Programs). 1993. *Human Development Report*. Oxford: Oxford University Press.

———. 1996. Human Development Report. Oxford: Oxford University Press.

———. 1998. Human Development Report. Oxford: Oxford University Press.

Williamson, John, ed. 1994. *The Political Economy of Policy Reform.* Washington, D.C.: Institute of International Economics.

World Bank. 1991. *World Bank Atlas 1991.* Washington, D.C.: World Bank.

———. 1996. *World Development Report 1996: From Plan to Market.* Washington, D.C.: World Bank; Oxford: Oxford University Press.

———. 1997a. *World Bank Atlas 1997.* Washington, D.C.: World Bank.

———. 1997b. *World Development Report 1997: The State in a Changing World.* Washington D.C.: World Bank; Oxford: Oxford University Press.

Table 1 Basic Demographic and Social Data on the Countries in Transition

Country	1995 Population (millions)	1985–1995 Pop. growth (%/year)	Life expectancy at birth (years) 1990	1995	Infant mortality rate per 1,000 live births 1991	1995	1994 Share of pop. age 15–64 (%)	Gini coeff. 1993 (%)	Gini coeff. Change since 1987–1988 (% pts.)	HDI[b] 1990	1995
Group One											
Czech Rep.	10.33	0.0	71.3[c]	73	10	8	65	27	8	0.892	0.884
Hungary	10.23	–0.3	69	70	16	11	62	23	2	0.887	0.857
Poland	38.61	0.4	71.1	70	15	14	55	30	5	0.831	0.851
Slovakia	5.37	0.3	70.9[c]	72	12	11	60	20[c]		0.892	0.875
Slovenia	1.99	0.1	n.a.[d]	74	10	7	56	28	4	n.a.	0.887
Bulgaria	8.40	–0.6	73	71	17	15	66	34	11	0.854	0.789
Romania	22.69	0.0	71	70	27	n.a.	65	26[c]		0.709	0.696
Estonia	1.49	–0.3	69.3	70	14	14	39	39	16	0.872	0.758
Latvia	2.52	–0.4	69.1	69	16	16	60	27		0.868	0.704
Lithuania	3.72	0.5	70.4	69	14	14	55	34		0.881	0.750
Albania	3.26	1.0	72	73	28	30	60	n.a.		0.699	0.656
Group Two											
Russia	148.20	0.3	67.9[c]	65	20	18	65	48	14–24[e]	0.862	0.769
Belarus	10.34	0.4	69.8[c]	70	15	13	60	22		0.861	0.783
Ukraine	51.55	0.1	69.4[c]	69	18	15	60	26[c]		0.844	0.665
Moldova	4.34	0.4	67.6[c]	69	23	22	60	34[c]		0.758	0.610

Kazakhstan	16.61	0.5	69.6[c]	69	32	27	59	33[c]		0.802	0.695
Kyrgyzstan	4.52	1.2	69[c]	68	40	30	55	50	9–33[e]	0.689	0.633
Turkmenistan	19.17	3.3	65[c]	67	56	46	55	36		0.726	0.660
Uzbekistan	22.77	2.3	69.2[c]	70	44	30	55	n.a.		0.695	0.659

SOURCE: World Bank 1991 and 1997a; World Bank 1996; UNDP, 1993 and 1996.

[a] The Gini index measures the extent to which the actual distribution of income deviates from a perfectly equal distribution. A Gini index of 0 percent represents a perfect equality, whereas an index of 100 percent represents maximum inequality.

[b] The HDI (Human Development Index) as computed by the United Nations Development Program.

[c] 1992 data.

[d] n.a. = data not available.

[e] A range of values for the change is due to statistical inconsistencies.

Table 2 Basic Macroeconomic Data on the Countries in Transition

Country	1995 GDP per capita[a] (U.S.$)	1995 GDP per capita PPP[b] (U.S.$)	GDP growth index[c] 1993[e]	GDP growth index[c] 1996	1995 Unemployment rate (% of labor force)	1995 Investment rate (% of GDP)	1995 Investment index[c]	Inflation rate[d] Highest (1991–1996)	Inflation rate[d] 1996	1996 Average monthly wages (U.S.$)	1995 General government balance/ GDP
Group One											
Czech Rep.	3,870	9,770	65.4	69.8	2.9	31.0	65	57 (1991)	9	356	0.4
Hungary	4,120	6,410	81.9	86.0	10.4	19.3	62	35 (1991)	24	307	–6.5
Poland	2,790	5,400	82.2 (1991)	104.5	14.9	17.1	55	586 (1990)	20	350	–3.5
Slovakia	2,950	6,660	75.0 (1992)	89.8	13.1	29.2	60	61 (1991)	6	266	3.2
Slovenia	8,200	9,350	79.9 (1992)	88.2	14.5	21.2	56	549 (1990)	10	953	–0.0[f]
Bulgaria	1,330	4,480	73.3	68.5	11.1	14.2	66	338 (1991)	123	77	–5.7
Romania	1,480	4,360	75.0 (1992)	88.2	9.5	21.9	65	256 (1993)	39	138	–2.8
Estonia	2,860	4,220	63.2 (1992)	67.0	15.0	25.0	39	1,078 (1992)	23	n.a.	–0.8
Latvia	2,270	3,370	51.0	51.7	6.6	16.6	60	951 (1992)	18	n.a.	–3.3
Lithuania	1,900	4,120	37.2	40.1	7.3	21.4	55	1,020 (1992)	25	n.a.	–3.3

Albania	670	n.a.	72.0	73.0	13.1	n.a.	60	193 (1992)	8	n.a.	–9.4
Group Two											
Russia	2,240	4,480	71.9	56.6	8.2	19.8	65	1,529 (1992)	48	156	–4.9
Belarus	2,070	4,220	78.2	63.4	2.7	25.1	60	2,220 (1994)	53	n.a.	–1.9
Ukraine	1,630	2,400	68.0	41.6	0.9	20.0	60	4,735 (1993)	24	75	–5.0
Moldova	920	n.a.	57.0	35.0	1.4	7.4	60	1,751 (1993)	24	n.a.	–5.5
Kazakhstan	1,330	3,010	49.0 (1995)	49.2	2.1	18.8	59	1,880 (1994)	39	n.a.	–2.3
Kyrgyzstan	700	1,800	53.2 (1995)	56.3	3.0	22.0	55	1,209 (1993)	30	n.a.	–12.5
Turkmenistan	920	n.a.	82.7	59.6	n.a.	n.a.	55	2,714 (1993)	500	n.a.	–1.6
Uzbekistan	970	2,370	80.5 (1995)	82.1	0.3	n.a.	55	550 (1994)	50	n.a.	–4.1

SOURCE: World Bank 1996; Podkaminer et al. 1998 (for monthly wages in $).

[a] Based on the 1995 exchange rate.

[b] PPP = purchasing power parity.

[c] 1989 = 100.

[d] Annual % change in CPI from preceding year.

[e] Or lowest point of the GDP index.

[f] Actual value –0.03.

[g] n.a. = data not available.

Table 3 Foreign Trade and Financial Data on the Countries in Transition

Country	1996 Foreign trade indicators		1996	FDI, cumulated		FDI cumulated	1996
	Import/GDP	Export/GDP ratio	Trade balance (% of GDP)	1988–1996 (U.S.$, millions)	1996 FDI flow (% of GDP)	1988–1996 per capita (U.S.$)	Gross debt (% of GDP)
Group One							
Czech Rep.	54.0	42.6	–11.5	7,371	2.7	712	36
Hungary	36.4	29.6	–6.9	13,377	4.5	1,307	62
Poland	28.2	18.6	–9.2	5.492	2.1	142	31
Slovakia	57.7	46.6	–11.1	789	0.3	147	33
Slovenia	50.8	44.9	–5.9	786	1.0	393	22
Bulgaria	43.3	45.3	2.0	399	0.9	48	103
Romania	28.1	21.6	–6.5	1,184	0.6	52	23
Estonia	75.3	48.9	–26.4	752	1.4	507	7
Latvia	45.4	28.3	–17.2	775	4.2	310	8
Lithuania	59.6	44.4	–15.2	261	1.5	70	16
Albania	34.8	8.1	–26.7	258	2.2	72	23
Group Two							
Russia	7.1	15.6	8.5	7,519	0.4	50	29
Belarus	17.6	13.6	–4.0	57	0.1	6	10
Ukraine	18.6	15.6	–3.0	1,245	0.9	24	20
Moldova	26.0	15.9	–10.1	167	5.7	38	41
Kazakhstan	6.2	13.9	7.7	2,591	5.0	150	n.a.

Kyrgyzstan	22.5	5.8	–16.7	n.a.	n.a.	n.a.	n.a.
Turkmenistan	30.6	17.7	–12.9	n.a.	n.a.	n.a.	n.a.
Uzbekistan	22.3	20.3	–2.1	n.a.	n.a.	n.a.	n.a.

SOURCE: EBRD 1996; ECE/UN 1997; World Bank 1991, 1996, and 1997a; Podkaminer et al. 1997.

Table 4 Structural Data on the Countries in Transition

Country[a]	Column 1 Priv./GDP[b] (%)	2 L–S priv.[c]	3 Enterpr. restr.[d]	4 Price lib.[e]	5 Forex lib.[f]	6 Comp. pol.[g]	7 Bank reform[h]	8 Capital markets[i]	Overall rating[j] (cols. 2–8)
Group One[j]									
Czech Rep.	75	4	3	3	5	3	3	3	24
Hungary	70	4	3	3	5	3	3	3	24
Poland	60	3	3	3	5	3	3	3	23
Estonia	70	4	3	3	4	3	3	2	22
Slovenia	45	3	3	3	5	2	3	3	22
Slovakia	70	3	3	3	5	3	3	3	23
Romania	60	3	2	3	3	1	3	2	17
Bulgaria	45	2	2	2	4	2	2	2	16
Latvia	60	3	3	3	4	2	3	2	20
Lithuania	65	3	3	3	4	2	3	2	20
Albania	75	2	2	3	4	2	2	2	17
Group Two									
Russia	60	3	2	3	4	2	2	3	19
Belarus	15	1	2	3	2	2	1	2	13
Ukraine	40	2	2	3	3	2	2	2	16
Moldova	40	3	2	3	4	2	2	2	18
Kazakhstan	40	3	2	3	4	2	2	2	18

Kyrgyzstan	50	3	2	3	4	2	2	2	18
Turkmenistan	20	1	1	2	1	1	1	1	8
Uzbekistan	40	3	2	3	2	2	2	2	16

SOURCE: Adapted from EBRD 1996; data as of August 1996.

[a] Countries in Group 1 are listed in general order of consideration for EU admission.

[b] Priv./GDP = officially declared share of the private sector in the creation of GDP.

[c] L-S priv. = large-scale privatization.

5: Standards typical of advanced industrial economies, though the state of corporate governance may be unclear; more than 75% of state assets privatized

4: More than 50% of state assets privatized; apparently substantial insider ownership

3: More than 25% of state assets privatized; apparently substantial insider ownership

2: Beginning of implementation of comprehensive privatization schemes

1: Little private ownership

[d] Enterpr. rest. = enterprise restructuring.

3: Significant and sustained actions to harden budget constraints and to enforce bankruptcy legislation

2: Moderately tight credit, weak enforcement of bankruptcy legislation; de-monopolization is slow

1: Soft budget constraint (lax tax and credit policies); few efforts to promote corporate governance

[e] Price lib. = price liberalization.

3: Substantial progress on price liberalization; energy prices, utilities not completely freed

2: Substantial remaining price controls and state procurement

[f] Forex lib. = foreign exchange liberalization.

5: Completed, with only some restrictions for capital movements

4: Quasi-convertibility of the domestic currency for current account transactions

3: Remaining exchange controls and multiple exchange rates

2: Some liberalization of import and export controls; almost full current account convertibility, but the forex regime is not transparent and may have multiple rates

1: Widespread export/import and foreign exchange controls

[g] Comp. pol. = competition policy.

3: Some efforts to promote a competitive environment; reduction of entry restrictions; difficulties in breaking up of large monopolies

2: Competition policies and institutions beginning to be set up

1: No competitive legislation or policy

[h] Bank. reform = banking reform.

3: Fully established two-tier system; framework for prudential regulation; significant presence of private or foreign banks, though the banking sector remains state-owned in its majority; beginning of a lending policy, though banks remain risk-adverse and lack experience in assessing the solvency of the enterprises, thus restraining credit and contributing to inter-enterprise arrears.

2: Liberalization of interest rates and credit allocation; limited use of directed credit or interest rate ceilings

1: Two-tier system; no further reform

[i] Capital markets.

3: Creation of investment vehicles (investment funds, insurance, or pension funds); opening of stock exchanges; issuance of securities by private enterprises and by the government

2: Legislation for the setting up of stock exchanges; some trading in government bonds

1: Little progress in reforms

[j] Overall rating.

The overall rating is a "mechanical" addition of ratings obtained in Columns 2 though 8. It is obvious that the provisional choice of the European Commission in selecting the first group of countries to begin negotiations for EU accession (confirmed by the December 1997 Summit of the EU) rests upon logical assumptions. Estonia is doing best among the Baltic states and Slovenia among the Southeast European ones (in addition, Slovenia has the highest GDP per capita of all the countries in transition [see Table 2], which would suggest less need for support). As to the "exclusion" of Slovakia, it has been motivated mainly by political reasons (the lack of respect for the rights of minorities, and what is felt in the West as the lasting influence of former Party and police cadres).

2 The End of Transition?

Alan Gelb
The World Bank

When is transition over? That question was frequently asked as we prepared the *1996 World Development Report: From Plan to Market*. We did come up with an answer. Transition is over when the problems and the policy issues confronted by today's "transition countries" resemble those faced by other countries at similar levels of development.

Why this answer? Is there not a more definitive benchmark? Some have suggested that transition ceases with membership in the European Union (EU). This Eurocentric approach, however, overlooks the vast differences between transition countries. The Czech Republic and China have little in common except that they were planned socialist countries dominated by the Communist Party. Vietnam's level of development is far from that of Hungary, and the latter is much more developed in economic and social terms than Turkmenistan. Such differences—and many others—have influenced countries' choice of transition paths and the outcomes from their reforms.

The differences are also important for the endpoints of transition. After the initial phases of liberalizing the controlled economy and attaining or maintaining macroeconomic stability, deep institutional change is essential for the transition process. Even comparing countries that have been market economies for long periods, formal market-supporting institutions are typically far stronger in those nations that are more developed and have higher income levels. Few poor countries have well-functioning legal systems, or effective, well-regulated financial markets. The extent to which institutional development needs to precede and set the stage for growth, rather than to simply follow rising income, is a debated question, and one can find examples suggesting an emphasis on one or the other of these sides. Nevertheless, the relationship between income levels and formal institutional development points to the fact that transition has different endpoints for the countries concerned as well as different starting points. Like automobiles, market economies come in many different models. The Democratic Republic of Congo (formerly Zaire) and Switzerland are each, in its own way, market economies.

Whatever the endpoint, transition countries are not there yet. Considering individual countries, we see features of their transition process that may extend out a long way into the future. The Czech voucher funds, for example, will provide a distinctive dimension to ownership for some time. Countries such as Romania and Armenia, which privatized agricultural land in small parcels to households, will need to undergo an extended period of consolidation to achieve a long-run equilibrium distribution of commercial landholding. The reverse is the case in countries such as Russia, where large state farms were transformed into huge joint-stock corporations, resulting in a distribution of landholding unlike that in any other market economy, where farms are on average far smaller and are usually owned by families, even if formally incorporated. In some countries, such as Poland, it will take time to resculpt the role of the state in social protection towards the patterns typical of the more industrial market economies—even as these patterns are themselves evolving.

To better focus on where the transition countries are relative to the "reform frontier," let us consider the following questions. How far have transition countries come along various dimensions of reform, and what has driven reforms in diverse groups of countries? How have differences between countries influenced the response to reforms? What is the remaining agenda for the countries in these groups? Transition is an ongoing process, and our evaluation of the reforms and their consequences must still be tentative—but we know a lot more than we did a few years ago.

MOVEMENT TO THE MARKET

Transition involves a lot more than freeing prices, but liberalization of the planned economy is at the core of the transition process. Here, we can consider three groups of countries: the advanced reformers in Central and Eastern Europe, the later reformers in the former

Soviet Union, and the East Asian cases, China and Vietnam. The first and third groups started reforms before the second, and, in addition, many in the first group of countries liberalized their economies very rapidly. Reforms, however, affect economies over a period of time rather than instantaneously and therefore need to be sustained: cumulative exposure to reforms is more important than the immediate situation. By 1996, as a result of these differences in speed and timing, the cumulative exposure to market forces since the initiation of reforms (that is, the number of reform-years expressed on a comparable basis) was perhaps twice as great for the more advanced of the reformers in Central and Eastern Europe than for typical countries in the former Soviet Union. The East Asian countries—despite the incomplete nature of their reforms—had also exposed their economies to market forces to a substantial extent.

Transition countries can also be compared along other policy dimensions: how far have they come, for example, in legal reform, in reducing the role of the state in production, in creating a market-based financial system, or in changing the social protection function of the state towards a role compatible with a market system? When this comparison is made, a broad pattern develops, suggesting that, in general terms, institutional evolution away from the planned model goes hand-in-hand with cumulative exposure to liberalized market forces. For example, no country has moved significantly towards creating a market-based financial system without sustained liberalization of the pricing mechanism for goods and services.

This broad parallelism between market and institutional reforms is not precise enough to determine the answer to all pressing policy dilemmas: for example, at what stage is it appropriate to liberalize financial markets? However, it does serve to show the limited value of the debate on whether market or institutional reforms should come first. Certainly, the efficiency of market economies reflects the strength of their underlying institutions, meaning that a sudden liberalization of markets risks pitchforking a planned economy into a very inefficient market mode of operation. Some analysts therefore argue that market reforms should only proceed after the institutional underpinnings of markets are present. Yet, market-supporting institutions cannot develop without clear demand for their services. Without market discipline and private creditors, for example, countries will not develop the capacity to administer bankruptcy laws; without private shareholders, the capacity to enforce minority ownership rights will remain undeveloped. Incomplete liberalization or attempts to sustain the status quo can also inhibit the development of market-supporting institutions: the case has been made, for example, against attempts to sustain the ruble zone rather than moving rapidly to a system of market-clearing national currencies in the former Soviet Union.

Thus, there are strong synergies and bidirectional causality chains between elements of the transition, so that, to be effective, reforms typically have to proceed across a fairly broad front. This interdependence of policies is one of the factors that distinguishes transition from the more normal process of selective policy reform within an established market system.

What, then, has driven reforms? The answer seems to be a mixture of three factors. The first is the steady decline in efficiency of the planned economy relative to market systems. Sharply falling productivity became evident in the Soviet Union in the early 1960s, and, by the end of the 1980s, the Soviet economy had essentially stalled, despite high investment rates. The quality of machinery exported from Eastern Europe to Western Europe declined steadily relative to that of machinery from market economies, as shown by a persistent fall in its value per unit of weight to a little over one-third of market economy levels. Propelled by a very high forced savings rate, China's growth was appreciable, yet, especially in rural areas, consumption lagged and living standards fell considerably behind those of the rapidly growing market economies in the region.

The second factor driving reform is political change. Across Central and Eastern Europe and the former Soviet Union, the timing and intensity of economic reforms, as measured by estimates of liberalization and other indicators, correlate closely with indicators of political change, as assessed by advances in civil liberties and political freedoms. Such change was perhaps the major driving force for reforms in Central and Eastern Europe, and it is no accident that economic reforms progressed faster in countries such as Estonia, Poland, and the Czech Republic, where political changes were the most radical. Fundamental political change created an opening for radical economic change, a so-called "period of extraordinary politics" devoid of effective pressure groups able to oppose the adverse impact that economic reforms would have on many established sectors and enterprises. In addition, optimism on the political side due to expectations of rejoining Western Europe provided an important stabilizer in the initial, difficult, transition years. Countries such as China and Uzbekistan, in contrast, were far less ready to subject the industrial core of the planned economic system to the full market forces unleashed by reforms.

Macroeconomic crisis is the third factor that has shaped the approach to reform and its speed. As tight political control and the planned economy began to erode in Central and Eastern Europe and the former Soviet Union, so macroeconomic imbalances grew. This situation was propelled forwards by weakening central controls on wages and on the investment demands of state enterprises, in the face of the limited supply of goods and services made available by the stagnating economy. Financial balances began to build up in household and enterprise savings accounts. Representing claims on resources that had been made available to the planned economy, these large involuntary holdings or "money overhangs" would have rendered attempts at slow liberalization very difficult, and they also had important inflationary consequences when prices were released. The money overhang was especially severe in the common ruble zone of the Soviet Union. It was significant in some of the Central and Eastern European countries but less so in others, and it was negligible in China, where, in contrast, households were underfinancialized at the start of reforms.

Because of the range of imbalances, the pace and phasing of reforms differed between countries. Driven by a combination of political changes and severe macro-imbalances, many countries in Central and Eastern Europe and the former Soviet Union initiated rapid liberalization programs, followed by fiscal and monetary policies aimed at stabilizing the price level. Inheriting high open inflation, reformers in Vietnam also initiated swift, if more limited, changes. China's reforms, in contrast, opened with quick steps to partially liberalize the rural economy and to decollectivize agriculture; thenceforth, changes were in phases and relatively cautious, encouraging the entry of new nonstate firms but sustaining the core of the previous, state-owned enterprise system.

REFORM OUTCOMES

In Central and Eastern Europe and the former Soviet Union, the typical response to liberalization was high inflation associated with sharp economic contraction. The extent of the latter is debatable; indexes of economic activity that overemphasized the shrinking heavy industrial sectors and underweighted the emerging small-scale manufacturing and service sectors imparted a negative bias. Nevertheless, the representative country recorded early output losses of 20–40 percent of gross domestic product (GDP) and inflation rates that peaked at several hundred percent, although there were wide variations around these figures. Not all of the output loss necessarily translated into welfare losses: heavy industry, especially that connected with the military sector, had been greatly overbuilt, and lost output was probably a social good rather than a calamity. Still, the sharp decline in major enterprises created severe stress for those working in the relevant sectors.

Three to four years after reforms, however, things looked rather different. Inflation had been contained and brought down to moderate levels in many countries, and an expanding private sector, heavily oriented to services, was growing rapidly enough to be capable of offsetting the continued contraction of state industry. In about half of the countries in Central and Eastern Europe and the former Soviet Union, private business accounted for over 50 percent of economic activity by 1995, a remarkable increase from its share of 10–15 percent only a few years earlier. This gain was due both to new entry and, in many countries, significant privatization of the state sector using a variety of mechanisms. After bottoming out, many economies were beginning to expand again. Notably, growth resumed more strongly, and inflation came down more rapidly, in countries that liberalized their economies most resolutely, while the turnaround was more delayed in countries reforming in a hesitant manner. From a structural perspective, by the mid 1990s the leading reformers in Central and Eastern Europe had begun to approach the distribution of economic activity characteristic of market systems.

In contrast with this U-shaped pattern, China and Vietnam experienced rapid growth from the start of their transition. These nations maintained inflation at moderately low levels (in Vietnam's case, after initially bringing it down from high levels).

What has shaped the varying response of transition countries to their reforms? Has it simply been different policies? Or, have the outcomes of reform reflected variations among countries in terms of their initial conditions? The differential impact of policies and initial conditions is still a contentious question, and econometric study to disentangle their effects is only now becoming possible. Nevertheless, elements of the story are starting to be clear.

Abstracting from the political dimension, the heavily industrialized countries in Central and Eastern Europe and the former Soviet Union faced a very difficult choice. If they liberalized their economies, major segments, including massively overbuilt industries, would be exposed as hopelessly uncompetitive. There would then be pressure to subsidize these industries, to sustain output, and especially to preserve jobs. Where would resources come from for subsidies? The state enterprises were themselves major sources of fiscal revenues. On the financial sector side, sharp price increases resulting from the pent-up money overhang would wipe out savings, reducing the willingness of economic agents to continue to supply resources through the banking system. Bringing inflation down to levels where markets could function effectively and private investment needed to "grow the new economy" would not be discouraged would therefore require decisive action to cut subsidies, which would be very difficult until the state severed its links with the enterprises and allowed market forces to operate freely. The choice, given severe structural imbalances and a monetary overhang, has therefore been either rapid liberalization followed by cutting state subsidies and stabilizing the economy, or an extended period of economic contraction while trying in vain to protect the old industrial sector.

The interaction between policies and performance was very different in China. With far smaller state employment in relative terms and no pent-up purchasing power, China was able to reap large efficiency gains from rural reforms. These were then channeled towards accelerating industrialization, both by supplying resources to construct new "township and village" industries and by creating a rapidly growing market for industrial goods. At the same time, high savings out of rising incomes could be directed to the state enterprises through the banking system, cushioning them against the steadily increased competition with the nonstate sector as nonagricultural markets were progressively liberalized. This protection gave even laggard Chinese enterprises more time to adjust but stored up a problem for the future in the form of a large volume of nonperforming loans in the banking system.

Could an alternative policy have worked in Central and Eastern Europe and the former Soviet Union? For example, suppose governments had first privatized a wide range of small assets to absorb the money overhang and at the same time had reimposed tight control on wages and investment to prevent excess demand from reemerging. This policy in turn might possibly have paved the way for a more controlled process of reform, with gains from the growth of new sectors offsetting steady losses and contraction of old ones. Such a scenario might have been possible in theory, although the large relative size of the overbuilt sectors and the painful institutional changes needed—for example, to reform Soviet-style agriculture—would have rendered it very difficult and perhaps no less painful than the process that actually took place. However, such a hypothetical process was out of the question in the face of the essential springboard of the transition in Central and Eastern Europe and the former Soviet Union: weakening governments, followed by the breakdown of the political system itself.

Within this broad sweep of experience, there have been other contrasting outcomes. Geography and history have played important roles: recovery is easier for a country such as the Czech Republic, which has long borders with rich market economies, than for the Kyrgyz Republic, isolated in Central Asia with most communications routes going through Russia. Russia itself has been slower to recover than expected. One reason may be that the energy sector was the major provider of subsidies to other sectors under the planned system: with liberalization, benefits to the energy sector have flowed into relatively few hands, widening the disparity in the distribution of income and fueling an increase in imports and an export of capital that has left poorly equipped light industry and agriculture behind. Widespread corruption and conflicts over corporate governance have also increased the barriers to private investment and growth. Perhaps we now have too many explanations for transition outcomes! But at least we understand the factors better, even if we do not know their exact relative weights in determining the results.

THE AGENDA TO COME

What of the future? What are the remaining issues on the reform agenda? Phase 1 reforms involving the introduction of market forces and the opening of economies to private firms are well on the way in all but the least advanced transition countries. Phase 2 reforms, including those of the legal system, of the financial system, and of government itself, involve institutional change as well as the virtual creation of new professions, such as lawyers, bank supervisors, and accountants capable of functioning in a market economy. The necessary institutional change runs deep, extending down into the educational systems of the transition countries as well as to courts, banks, and governments themselves. Therefore, it cannot be a rapid process.

At the risk of generalization, the reform agenda can be discussed according to the three groups of countries. All have a great deal of economic promise. Central and Eastern European countries can benefit from "catch-up" with their large, rich, market-economy neighbors. The former Soviet Union can exploit an abundant natural-resource and human-capital base far more effectively than hitherto. The crises of late 1997 notwithstanding, the East Asian transition countries also have strong bases to tap, including a hardworking, educated population, a tradition of high saving, and proximity to a region with high long-run growth potential. Yet, to achieve their potential as market economies, all three groups face major challenges.

The leading reformers in Central and Eastern Europe are well along with Phase 1 changes. Phase 2 includes harmonization with the EU in preparation for accession. The primary challenge remaining is to reduce the role of the state in their economies to the point where this does not constitute a serious constraint on competitiveness and growth. State spending, largely for social programs and, in particular, pensions, still comprises close to 50 percent of GDP in some of the countries, as large as before transition. This high share has been sustained by a heavy, and distorting, tax structure that, among other things, creates a strong disincentive to hire labor through the formal economy. Competitor countries at similar income levels, including those in the Far East, impose substantially lower fiscal burdens on their productive sectors, making space for far higher levels of investment.

The challenge in much of the former Soviet Union is very different. The collapse of the Soviet Union seriously undermined the capability and the credibility of governments. Fiscal revenues fell sharply, and governments lost effectiveness in administering law and order as well as in the area of social protection. The credibility of Russia's policy regime, as viewed through a survey of businesses, ranked with the poorest in the world and fell far short of that viewed as prevailing in the Czech Republic. In some cases in the former Soviet Union, property rights have been reallocated towards the private sector on a massive scale, as in Russia, but the distributional and corporate governance consequences of the mechanisms used have been contentious. In some cases, as in agriculture, formal privatization has not yet led to an effective reallocation of rights towards individuals. Reforms in the former Soviet Union are therefore at a more elemental state than in the more advanced countries in Central and Eastern Europe.

Despite very rapid growth, China faces a pressing set of issues, including a massive deferred agenda of urban reforms. These include changes in the social security system (even in the late 1990s, Chinese enterprises are still largely responsible for pensions, housing, and healthcare, making it difficult to close them down) and the banking system, which is burdened by a massive "black hole" of nonperforming loans. The announcement of a $35 billion bond issue in February 1998 suggests an approach towards the problem posed by the stock of bad loans; however, measures to stem the flow of new bad loans would have severe implications for many enterprises that depend on continued lending. Some 100 million workers in nonstate firms are outside the formal social system yet no longer tied to agriculture; a "floating population" of some 70 million has broken down previous constraints on labor mobility. In addition, the state's ability to redistribute resources from growing coastal provinces towards poor remote regions needs to be restored; central government's fiscal revenues have fallen throughout the reform period, reaching low shares of GDP by the mid 1990s.

Finally, let us consider social factors arising from transition that may affect post-transition performance. Experience so far suggests that the process of transition is not easily reversed. Even the return of ex-socialists to power in certain countries in Central and Eastern Europe and the former Soviet Union has not caused the economic reform clock to be turned back, although it has, in some cases, slowed the pace of change. What kinds of economies and societies will the transition countries turn out to be? Will the distribution of property emerge as sharply unequal? Property rights to large assets have been difficult to disperse rapidly on a wide scale, except perhaps through the use of voucher schemes as implemented in the Czech Republic. Yet experience shows that, if formal property rights are not allocated rather early in the transition, they tend to become appropriated anyway by powerful individuals or groups as the hold of the state on the economy weakens. Related to this question is that of the social and economic impact of increasing income inequality. From initially low or moderate levels, Gini coefficients[1] have tended to increase for most countries in transition, somewhat in Central and Eastern Europe and sharply in the former Soviet Union. Cross-country studies of market economies suggest that nations with highly unequal income distributions perform relatively poorly, in part because distributional concerns fuel social tensions that cause policies to be less stable. Here is a major challenge for many of the transition countries in the future.

NOTES

NOTE: The material for this lecture is based on the World Bank *World Development Report 1996: From Plan to Market* (Oxford: Oxford University Press) and associated research. The lecture, however, expresses the views of the author. It does not necessarily represent the views of the World Bank, its executive directors, or the countries that they represent.

1. The Gini coefficient is a measure of the inequality of income distribution.

3 The End of Rent-Seeking

The End of Postcommunist Transformation

Anders Åslund
Carnegie Endowment for International Peace

During the last seven years, 27 countries in Eastern Europe and the former Soviet Union have departed from communism and attempted to build some kind of a market economy. Initially, the prescriptions presented by mainstream economists sounded rather similar in essence, although there was a great deal of debate over sequencing and speed.

Today, the most striking observation is how differently various postcommunist countries have fared. Poland returned to economic growth in 1992, and its total decline is now considered to have been less than 10 percent of gross domestic product (GDP). Other Central European countries experienced only slightly greater decreases. Most post-Soviet republics, on the contrary, have faced a drop from their prior GDP of 40–50 percent even by optimistic estimates, and several have still not returned to economic growth.

How can we explain these great differences? The theoretical economics literature on transition has focused particularly on the costs of structural adjustment and how to minimize them. The fundamental idea has been for policy to establish an optimal trade-off between various costs. However, the very large declines in GDP can hardly be considered results of any structural adjustment.

The most straightforward explanatory variable is inflation, and the degree and duration of inflation are, in turn, best explained by the degree and duration of rent-seeking. Inflation is largely caused by rent-seeking, which tends to be financed though the state budget, either through direct subsidies, such as price subsidies, or through hidden ones, such as subsidized credits issued by the central bank or exchange rate subsidies financed by foreign credits. Ultimately, these various subsidies derive from the state budget, but more transparent ones, such as direct budget subsidies, do tend to be less significant, as it is hard to defend them in any open political process.

The main drama of the postcommunist transformation in my eyes has been the strife between those who want to minimize rent-seeking and those who want to maximize it. Those who want to maximize it have benefited personally from the huge rents of the transition. Their very aim has been rent-seeking, that is, the extraction of monetary benefits from the government, either directly through subsidies or indirectly through government regulations often connected with quasi-fiscal expenditures. The opposite of rent-seeking is profit-seeking in a competitive market. In some countries, notably Russia, parts of the government have tried to contain rent-seeking, while other forces both inside and outside of government have tried to maximize rent-seeking. Increasingly, it becomes evident that rent-seeking is the key problem after communism.[1]

The main tasks of postcommunist transformation are all related to rent-seeking. A great deal of this behavior is caused by arbitrage between usually low, regulated state prices and higher free-market prices at home or abroad, an opportunity resulting from regulation of prices and exportation. Privatization is the most contentious issue. Many see it as the essence of rent-seeking (Goldman 1994; Nelson and Kuzes 1995), while others, including me, would rather consider it the end of rent-seeking (Kaufmann and Siegelbaum 1996).

In order to clarify the type of rent-seeking I am addressing, I shall first detail the main forms of rents in the Russian transition and assess their size and development. Curiously, rent-seeking has shrunk considerably, and the main question of this paper is to clarify how and why rent-seeking has waned. In doing so, I broaden the spectrum to the whole region, to offer an understanding of why this change has occurred in various countries.

THE NATURE OF POSTCOMMUNIST RENT-SEEKING

When communism was collapsing, the Union of Soviet Socialist Republics (USSR) was a paradise for rent-seeking. Large fortunes could be made in no time thanks to connections and ruthlessness. The methods were many, but three were particularly important. Today, we can establish both the techniques and the amounts involved.

The fundamental method of rent-seeking was arbitrage: to buy cheaply anything at fixed state prices and to sell at a high free-market price. The great spree of arbitrage occurred in 1991 and 1992, when raw materials, notably oil, natural gas, and metals, sometimes cost less than 1 percent of the world market price. Traders who had access to these commodities in Russia and were able to sell them abroad made untold fortunes in a few deals. Considering domestic and world market prices and the volume of exports, total rents arising from the sales abroad of oil, gas, and metals amounted to about 30 percent of Russia's GDP in 1992.[2] The export rents were particularly large in Russia, because of its large sales of raw materials and semimanufactured goods such as metals, but even Ukraine had huge rents from exports of underpriced metals.

A second major source of rents was import subsidies. They arose from multiple exchange rates, allowing another kind of arbitrage. In 1992, an importer paid only 1 percent of the official exchange rate for the hard currency needed to import essential foods, and that year no less than 15 percent of Russian GDP went to import subsidies (International Monetary Fund 1993, pp. 132–183, 140). These import subsidies were financed off the budget with Western commodity credits and did not show up in the Russian budget. Yet, the Russian state is responsible for servicing and paying back these international credits. In Ukraine, gas imports have continued to be a major source of rent-seeking. Until the end of 1994, oil and gas imports were subject to privileged exchange rates. In effect, Ukraine's gas importers' privileges were financed by Russia's natural gas company Gazprom, as nonpayments to Gazprom made up the bulk of Ukraine's large debt to Russia.[3]

A third form of rent to the privileged was subsidized credits, which were huge throughout the ruble zone in 1992 and 1993. When prices were liberalized in January 1992, money became scarce, as the money supply did not rise as fast as prices. The state enterprises urged the government and the central bank to replenish their working capital. Unfortunately, the government and the central bank tried to accommodate this request. From June until September 1992, the Russian money supply increased by almost 30 percent a month. Worse, most of these credits were issued at highly subsidized interest rates, at 10 or 25 percent per annum, while inflation was 2,500 percent that year. Thus, the credits were virtual gifts from the state to the receiving enterprises.

The total volume of credit subsidies amounted to some 30 percent of GDP in 1992, but initially these sums were not included in the state budget.[4]

Even so, Russia had less credit issue than most post-Soviet states. Table 1 presents the net issue of credit in various countries in 1992. The subsidization of credits was almost as large as the net issue of credit, as very low nominal interest rates prevailed at the time. We can note that the amount of subsidized credits was larger in several other former Soviet republics than in Russia in 1992, while it was much less in the Baltic states. In 1993, Russia put its credit issue under some control and ended up with an inflation of "only" 840 percent, while the other former Soviet republics continued with very high credit issue, leading to hyperinflation in 10 of them.

Incredibly, we can conclude that gross rents from these three sources alone amounted to about 75 percent of GDP in Russia in 1992. The situation varied from country to country, but these three forms of rent were strongly developed in the whole of the former Soviet Union. None of these rents can be defended from any social point of view, but they were technically legal. Little wonder that people had a perception of lawlessness. Moreover, the division of the spoils involved a great

Table 1 Net Revenues from Credit Issue in Post-Soviet Countries, 1992

Country	% of GDP
Estonia	0.2
Latvia	11.9
Lithuania	19.7
Kyrgyz Republic	29.1
Moldova	32.6
Russia	32.7
Ukraine	34.5
Kazakhstan	35.7
Belarus	42.8
Turkmenistan	63.2

SOURCE: Åslund, Boone, and Johnson 1996 (p. 257).

deal of violent crime, particularly noticed in metal exports but also true in the distribution of subsidized credits.

The conventional wisdom is that the great fortunes in Russia were made through the voucher privatization, which largely benefited the managers of what were previously state enterprises. However, scrutiny of the numbers does not support this perception. By July 1997, the Russian stock market had reached a total market capitalization of about $100 billion, after having quintupled in 15 months.[5] This market capitalization included most of the value in the Russian enterprise sector, notably some 17,000 enterprises subject to voucher privatization, while real estate and small and new enterprises were not included. At the time, Russia's GDP was about $450 billion. In other words, all the fruits of the Russian voucher privatization were worth 22 percent of GDP in 1997. However, of this total figure, enterprise managers possessed only about 20 percent (Blasi, Kroumova, and Kruse 1997). That is, the enterprise managers' total gain from privatization after all of the price increases in the stock market was as little as 4.5 percent, while the total rents from the three sources discussed for the years 1991–1993 exceeded the GDP of one year.

In other countries, the direct rents from privatization were even less. Beside Russia, Poland has the largest market capitalization in what was the Soviet bloc, and it was only $12 billion in July 1997. Most of the other former Soviet republics privatized much less and later than Russia, but, according to the World Bank, the Kyrgyz Republic had even larger income differentials than Russia in 1993, although it had barely started its privatization then (World Bank 1996, p. 68).

While the direct benefits to managers from privatization were comparatively limited, much of rent-seeking, notably the export rents, involved management embezzlement of enterprise profits, which a strong owner would put an end to. Moreover, privatization implies the depoliticization and mostly deconcentration of ownership and the division between enterprises and state. Hence, strong alliances are often broken up, particularly if independent enterprises start competing on the market, and transparency also increases. Thus, privatization is likely to contribute to the end of rent-seeking, even if the very process of privatization may involve a limited amount of rent-seeking.

The significance to personal wealth of rent-seeking versus privatization becomes even more evident if we identify the social groups that are perceived as particularly rich in Russia. The first group consists of bankers, but most of the banks are new creations (Dmitriev et al. 1996). Clearly, the bankers' benefits were not so much from bank privatization as from subsidized credits and export rents. The second group comprises the oil and gas barons, who made their fortunes on export rents from 1991 through 1993: only in 1994 did their enterprises start being privatized. A third group is commodity traders, who thrived on both export rents and import subsidies.

In Ukraine, the metal exporters and the gas importers are the notably rich people, and in neither industry did any privatizations take place until 1997. Consistently, Ukrainians do not share the Russian view that privatization has benefited the newly rich in business. Thus, the evidence suggests that privatization does not lead to primary rent-seeking. It is another matter that those who already have money can buy assets and advance themselves further.

To conclude, a relatively small group has profited enormously from the rent-seeking that arose during the end of communism and the birth of capitalism in Russia. The foremost rents have been export rents, subsidized credits, and import subsidies. They have been strongly concentrated in the hands of some state enterprise managers and early commercial operators in trade and finance. In contrast to profits, these rents have been extracted thanks to privileged access and corruption rather than from competition on a free market. The rents have been shaped by state regulations that have effectively favored the privileged. Privatization has hardly contributed to this process.

WHY WAS RENT-SEEKING SO LARGE IN THE FORMER SOVIET UNION?

The general impression is that rent-seeking has been far greater in Russia than elsewhere. However, the same conditions that apply to Russia are largely true of the other former Soviet republics, save the Baltic states. The contrast is rather between the former Soviet republics and East-Central Europe. There are many reasons why rent-seeking was worse in the former Soviet republics. The causes were both economic and political. To a considerable extent, the severity of rent-seeking was the curse of the communists. The communists abolished private ownership in order to make the transition to socialism irreversible, but if there had been private ownership of the means of production, rent-seeking would have been much more limited.

The fundamental problem was political, namely, that the Soviet system created a small elite, about 1 percent of the population, that was virtually omnipotent. This elite controlled all levers of power and faced few restraints. In the old days, the system regulated itself, not by law, but through the Communist Party, its control organs, and the KGB. These mechanisms could not possibly be reconciled with a democratic state, the rule of law, or a market economy. Therefore, the controls had to go with the demise of communism and left the old communist elite more unrestrained than ever.

The postcommunist state was very weak. The absence of all kinds of normal institutions—political, market, economic, and legal—meant that few formal restrictions were at hand. Communism was contemptuous of the rule of law and tried to erase it. Instead, the Nomenklatura, the communist elite, was a law unto itself. The people with the best connections and the strongest will won regardless of the moral standards they represented. This situation fits well with Mancur Olson's logic of collective action. In an atomized society such as Russia, small groups with a lot at stake were likely to be the best organized and most effective (Olson 1971). It was obvious that wild rent-seeking would arise with the end of communism and that this rent-seeking could really be considered a "poison pill" planted by the communists, that is, a trap ensuring that the costs of abandoning communism would be great. The weakness of the postcommunist state was undoubtedly greater in the Soviet Union than in East-Central Europe, because Soviet communism lasted longer and was more ruthless.

Another problem with the postcommunist state was that democracy was weak. There is a strong correlation between political regime and economic reform strategy. Only democracies ruled by liberal governments attempted radical reforms, while all of the socialist governments, democratic or not, opted for gradual reforms initially (Åslund, Boone, and Johnson 1996, pp. 223–225). It was natural that the socialist governments chose gradual reforms, because these led to the most rent-seeking, which was in the interest of the strongest members of the old elite. That only some of the democratic regimes opted for radical reforms can be explained partly by new leaders not understanding the problems they faced (which is also reflected in the Western debate over postcommunist transformation), and partly by corrupt interests of the leaders. As the Central Asian countries show, dictatorships do appear to indulge in more rent-seeking. Hence, the idea that enlightened dictatorship should be beneficial to postcommunist transition seems misplaced, as any postcommunist dictatorship by necessity would control huge state resources, while being subject to little or no restriction.[6] Conversely, the stronger democracies in Central Europe (e.g., Poland, Czech Republic, and Hungary) and the Baltic countries (Estonia, Latvia, and Lithuania) did a great deal to eliminate rent-seeking at an early stage.

An additional political factor that influences rent-seeking is the strength of civil society. Unfortunately, in the postcommunist state, civil society has largely been very weak and could therefore do little to restrain rent-seeking. The foremost exception is Poland. Its strong trade unions, workers' councils, Catholic Church, and private peasants were vehemently against radical reform, but, by checking the powers of state enterprise managers and local officials, they managed to rein in rent-seeking early so that it was barely perceived as a major problem. Workers' councils also existed in Hungary, where they had some power, while those in the former Soviet Union disappeared without any significant impact.

Wherever the media's quality and independence were sufficient, it exerted beneficial pressures on rent-seekers. Again, the Central Europe and Baltic countries came out well, but Russia also benefited from strong media of high quality and independence from government, although much of the media has now fallen into the hands of some of the new major rent-seekers. At the same time, strong criticism by the Russian media has led to the misperception in many places that the problems in Russia are worse, while the point is rather that they are better known.

Thus, the overall power of the old elite over the rest of society differed between the regions of the former Soviet bloc, and with that the rent-seeking varied. I do not possess an overall measure of the extent of rent-seeking in the transition, but the height and duration of inflation are a good proxy, as most rent-seeking was eventually financed through the state budget and thus boosted the budget deficit. By that standard, the Commonwealth of Independent States (CIS) suffered particularly badly from rent-seeking, and Central Asia, Caucasus, and Ukraine most of all. Note that most CIS states were worse off than Russia. The Balkans followed next, as illustrated by the inflation crisis in Bulgaria and Romania as late as 1997. The Baltics have actually done better than those Balkan states, while the four Visegrad countries (Czech Republic, Hungary, Poland, and Slovakia) and Slovenia form a category of their own with relatively little suffering.

There were also strong economic grounds for the prevalence of rent-seeking. The situation was aggravated by the nature of the communist economic system, which was really a form of kleptocracy. The command economy in its ideal form did not work, and most market economic adjustments were formally illegal. Hence, the custom developed to steal whatever you could, and the limit was set by repression rather than by law. An old anecdote ran, "Which is the richest country in the world? The Soviet Union, because everybody has been trying to steal as much as they can since 1917, and there is still plenty to steal." An important reason why the collapse of communism was so peaceful was that the old elite had split into an ideological hard core and an economically oriented group that wanted to abandon communism for personal economic gains. However, the latter did not really want a competitive market economy. They preferred an intermediary stage in which they could keep control over economic assets, benefiting from a multitude of market distortions, while not suffering from the hardship of market competition. Naturally, these tendencies were worse in the Soviet Union than in East-Central Europe due to the duration and severity of communism; the same was true of more specific economic causes.

In the former Soviet Union, there were no market economic standards of any kind, and economic distortions were extraordinary. The relative prices were particularly perverse, with domestic prices sometimes less than 1 percent of world prices in 1991 at the market exchange rate. The greater the discrepancy between domestic prices and world prices, the greater the arbitrage, and the more distorted the relative prices were, the stronger the resistance against price liberalization. Interest rates had played no role in the Soviet system, and no capital or credit markets existed.

Another form of extortion was the wholesale trading system of the former Soviet Union, which to a considerable extent was based on politics rather than on economic calculation. Transportation costs were disregarded, while hauls could be enormous. Thus, many economic activities could not be justified if based on market pricing. In addition, defense expenditures probably comprised about one-quarter of GDP towards the end of the Soviet Union, while they have fallen to about 3 percent in postcommunist Russia. Thus, some 22 percent of GDP became redundant.

Another economic cause of massive rent-seeking was the deep financial crisis that all postcommunist countries but Hungary and Czechoslovakia faced at the end of communism; this crisis was particularly severe in the former Soviet Union. One of its aspects was a huge deficit of possibly up to 30 percent of GDP in 1991; another was that the Soviet Union defaulted on its foreign debt obligations in 1991, which in turn led to an extremely low free exchange rate. The budget deficit was financed with a huge monetary emission, and inflation skyrocketed as soon as prices were liberalized. The low exchange rate further intensified the problems of price liberalization, while it increased the opportunities for rents.

Finally, the larger the natural resource endowment, the greater the natural rent, and the richer the opportunities for rent-seeking, particularly in exports. This situation points to more opportunities for rents in the oil- and gas-rich countries—Russia, Kazakhstan, Azerbaijan, and Turkmenistan—which coincides with our perception of reality. It is not by chance that some of the largest fortunes in Russia appear to have been amassed in the oil and gas sectors. There are now a number of billionaires, and, at least until 1996, these were created by trade rather than by management privatization.

A combined political and economic reason for the lack of restraints on rent-seeking in the former Soviet Union was the extraordinary public ignorance of what a market economy really meant. Therefore, the rent-seekers could get away with all kinds of arguments that were unacceptable in East-Central Europe. There was no understanding whatsoever of capital and credit markets or that interest should reflect a justified price of capital. For example, Russian industrialists were up in arms when the central bank raised the official refinance rates from 50 to 80 percent in the spring of 1992, while inflation that year amounted to 2,500 percent. Their argument ran that no Western country had such a high (nominal) interest rate, saying nothing about how no Western country had such large negative real interest rates. Similarly, post-Soviet public opinion reflected the conviction in 1992 that monetary emission and large budget deficits stimulated production. The concepts of fiscal and monetary restraints were not only unknown, but disdained. Indeed, inflation was thought of as stimulating production, and many old Soviet economists spoke of the necessity of living with hyperinflation for some time.

Marxist production fetishism remained very strong. Hence, many were against full liberalization of trade, because they argued that it would not give any increased output, not realizing that the very allocation of production is vital for the functioning of an economic system. As newly appointed prime minister, Viktor Chernomyrdin argued that Russia did not need any "bażaar." The production fetishism also led to weird perceptions of value, for example, that smokestacks were worth fortunes while real estate and land were worth little. Even if a majority was in favor of private property, popular biases prevailed against some kinds of individual ownership, notably of large enterprises and financial institutions.

A conviction persisted that Russia was dominated by large production monopolies, which, according to the elite, justified far-reaching control of trade; on the contrary, the real problem was trade monopolies, which could only be checked through extensive liberalization of trade (Brown, Ickes, and Ryterman 1994). Similarly, it was argued that Russia lacked "market infrastructure" and therefore could not withstand a swift deregulation of trade.

The lack of economic understanding aroused an unjustified fear of massive unemployment, while the true dilemma was poverty caused by excessively hesitant economic policies that led to high inflation. Similarly, there was a very human fear that fast changes would be detrimental, while the opposite was actually true. Characteristically, virtually all of these obscurantist arguments favored gradual or no changes and thus the rent-seekers.

It does appear highly plausible that rents have been greater in Russia than elsewhere. These arguments, apart from resource endowments, apply equally well to all CIS states, so I am not focusing on a primarily Russian situation. Only the Baltics have escaped many of the problems.

HOW RENT-SEEKING HAS BEEN REDUCED

Today, these blatant forms of rent-seeking have largely ceased. The only postcommunist countries that have not put their economies in elementary order with tenable macroeconomic stability are Belarus, Turkmenistan, and Tajikistan. Rent-seeking raged from 1991 to 1993 and has subsided since. The reduction of rent-seeking tells us a great deal about what was really important in the transition from a command economy to a market economy.

Technically, it was easy to abolish rent-seeking. Only a few fundamental measures were undertaken. In order to eliminate arbitrage, it was necessary to apply three measures: to decontrol all prices, to liberalize both domestic and foreign trade, and to unify the exchange rate. Largely, all of this has been accomplished in most CIS countries, although corruption and many minor but harmful regulations remain. Dishonest officials at all levels defend regulations in order to extort bribes.

Interest subsidies were abolished in the fall of 1993 in Russia and in most CIS states in 1994. Most countries have had high positive real interest rates since then. The standing of the central banks has been strengthened; some have obtained statutory independence, and all pursue firmer monetary policies. As a result of the abolition of subsidized credits, exchange rates have stabilized. The opportunities for rent-seeking or easy money in banking have largely disappeared.

As a consequence of all of these measures, gross rents have fallen sharply. In Russia, gross rents probably dropped to about 10 percent of GDP at the end of 1995 from over 75 percent of GDP in 1992. In other CIS countries, a similar development took place, although the peak must have varied considerably. The remaining rent-seeking came primarily from other sources: state guarantees, budget subsidies, and monopoly rents, while a small amount of export rent persisted. In other countries, such as Belarus and Ukraine, import rents have continued to be prominent.

The larger and more interesting issue, however, is the political economy of reducing rent-seeking. How was it possible to cut this misappropriation so swiftly? The rent-seekers had acquired great economic and political power. In many countries, they ran the government, while they held the government hostage in others. How could the behavior be changed so significantly in just a few years in most of the countries concerned? Fortunately, there have turned out to be many ways, both political and economic, of eliminating rents.[7]

The best approach is undoubtedly a swift and comprehensive radical reform, as a broad economic literature has long argued (Lipton and Sachs 1990). The former Polish minister of finance made the point that the government has a period of grace, a period of extraordinary politics, when out of idealism the population accepts a great deal of change. That is when as much economic reform as possible should be implemented (Balcerowicz 1994). This timing was achieved in Poland, the Czech Republic, Estonia, and, to a reasonable extent, in Latvia and Lithuania.

Even when initial overall reforms have failed, partial reforms have still turned out to be surprisingly successful in the elements that were introduced. In general, few policy reversals have occurred. For example, there was no going back after Deputy Prime Minister Yegor Gaidar succeeded in deregulating prices in Russia in January 1992. After he and Minister of Finance Boris Fedorov abolished subsidized credits in September 1993, there were hardly any calls for new subsidized credits. Similarly, after Ukraine unified the exchange rate at the end of 1994, no opposition was heard. The success of partial reforms is somewhat surprising, considering that partial reforms usually failed under communism (Kornai 1992). Presumably, the conviction of the inevitability of a market economy was strong enough to break some resistance, and after one market economic norm had been adopted, that approach started reinforcing itself. In the public mind, the new norm became the natural standard, and, as some economic interests started benefiting from the policy, they defended it.

Over time, it becomes easier to attack rents simply because they tend to decline. There are many reasons for this. The inflation tax decreases, as people and enterprises realize that money is not a true store of value during high inflation, and they keep increasingly less, which in turn leads to a greater velocity of money. Foreign trade rents shrink, as the initial, very low exchange rates appreciate in real terms, and extreme price distortions are simply too expensive to maintain, so that any government has to reduce them. Eventually, no government can finance a large budget deficit by any means after even the inflation tax has been reduced, and, with other expenditure cuts, rents have to be reduced. The gradual decline in rents might be an important reason why the resistance against radical economic change is so great at the beginning of a reform effort. The early opposition exists, not only because people do not understand reforms and fear the unknown, but also because the rent-seekers benefit the most then. Later on, they may let the rents go. This timing of rents largely explains why the same postcommunist regime in Moldova suddenly switched to a radical economic reform policy in 1994, after having won an election campaign by promising gradual reform.

Privatization has often been discussed as a form of rent-seeking but should instead be seen as a primary means of its termination (Kaufmann and Siegelbaum 1996). There are numerous reasons why this should be the case. First of all, privatization introduces real owners, who tend to be concerned about their enterprises (Boycko, Shleifer, and Vishny 1995). Ludwig von Mises' old dictum holds true: the very foundation for profit-seeking is often considered to be private ownership. Privatization implies depoliticization and individualization of enterprises. Moreover, as state enterprises need massive restructuring, suffer from underinvestment, and are usually badly managed, their assets comprise a finite resource that is not likely to be more than one-tenth of GDP in the early stages of the transition. Thus, in hindsight, it is difficult to understand all of the concern about the privatization of large enterprises, as so little value was actually involved. Kazakhstan turned to radical reform policies in late 1994 and stuck to them, partly because of shrinking rents and partly because of swift insider privatization.

Ultimately, rent-seeking leads to steep falls in output and in the standard of living. Therefore, rent-seekers tend to be unable to cheat the voters for long if democracy is being maintained. Elections have repeatedly ousted regimes of rent-seekers and engineered more radical economic reforms, notably in Ukraine in July 1994, in Romania in November 1996, and in Bulgaria in April 1997. Alas, if there is no democracy, this important method of correction is missing. Telling examples are Belarus, Turkmenistan, and Tajikistan.

Rent-seeking does not only reduce output but usually causes a financial crisis, which means that tax revenues shrink, and the government has to cut the budget. This crisis is normally part of the reason for sounder economic policies. It illustrates how important it is that the international community not be bankrolling countries that pursue bad economic strategies. A good current example is how Russia, or rather Gazprom, has been allowing Belarus in particular to run up large arrears.

When a financial crisis arises, most countries have nowhere to turn but to the International Monetary Fund (IMF), which ordains its standard economic policies: deregulation of prices and trade, which eliminates price subsidies; a positive real interest rate and the abolition of all interest subsidies; a unification of the exchange rate, which does away with import subsidies; a limited budget deficit; and restrained monetary expansion. All of these measures serve to abolish rent-seeking, and because the IMF provides substantial financing up front, it has great clout.

Finally, people need a broad understanding of what a market economy is and what it is not, so that they realize what rent-seeking is and how much it costs them. In the end, sizable rent-seeking can only be maintained with political repression, and even so it has to be relatively limited, as the available sources of financing run dry.

THE END OF TRANSITION IS THE END OF RENT-SEEKING

In hindsight, it is evident that postcommunist transformation has largely been a question of controlling rent-seeking. The earlier that has been done, the sooner a country has returned to economic growth. Rent-seeking was enormous in the countries of the CIS but much less in East-Central Europe. There were many political and economic reasons for the extraordinary rent-seeking in the post-Soviet countries, but they essentially involved the lack of restrictions on a small elite left behind by communism. The damage caused by rent-seeking has been huge, but it has, after all, diminished sharply within a few years. A key issue is that large rents naturally become impossible to finance in the long run; also they are not politically sustainable.

Russia's financial crisis, which culminated with both devaluation of the ruble and default on government debt obligations in August 1998, can serve as an illustration. In Russia, the rent-seekers thrived on partial reforms in 1992 (Hellman 1998), but soon rents started declining. Russia had become highly pluralist and competitive. Therefore, the competition over rents intensified, which drove down rents further (Shleifer and Vishny 1993). The financial crisis reflected a desperate competition over declining rents, extreme short-sightedness of the rent-seekers, and their total absence of social conscience. The collapse itself reduced the few remaining rents further and may very well have laid a new base for more radical and thus more socially oriented reforms in Russia, although the rents might still reappear in other forms.

NOTES

1. I made a first attempt to sort out rent-seeking in Russia in Åslund (1996, pp. 12–16). This paper owes a great deal to my collaboration with Peter Boone and Simon Johnson (Åslund, Boone, and Johnson 1996), to whom I express my gratitude.
2. In 1992, more than 70 percent of Russia's exports were subject to export quotas (Aven 1994, p. 84). Total Russian exports outside of the Commonwealth of Independent States (CIS) amounted to $42.4 billion that year (Goskomstat 1994, p. 3). The average domestic price of these regulated exports was at most 10 percent of the world market price, and export tariffs actually collected amounted to about $2.4 billion. GDP was only $80 billion at the market-determined exchange rate in 1992 (Åslund 1995, pp. 145–152, 197). Hence, export rents were 70 percent of $42.4 billion times 90 percent, minus $2.4 billion, which equals $24.3 billion. Considering that GDP was $80 billion, export rents were almost exactly 30 percent of GDP. (Export rents were particularly high in 1992 because of the very low exchange rate, which meant that exports appeared expensive in relation to the GDP.) Much of the capital flight arose from export rents. For instance, an export delivery was heavily underinvoiced, that is, officially sold below the market price, but resold abroad at the market price, and the Russian exporters put the difference in their bank accounts abroad. The export statistics have been revised upwards to compensate for such underinvoicing.
3. After the privileged exchange rates were gone, state guarantees effectively subsidized gas importers, and when they were finally gone in 1996, gas importers simply benefited from monopoly rents. In addition, these individuals refused to pay others, while they insisted on being paid themselves.

4. Granville (1995, p. 67). This is not to say that all the rents were to the rich and powerful. Layard and Richter (1994, pp. 459–471) discuss the transfers between different sectors of the economy (enterprises and households), but the benefits of the rent-seekers cannot be identified with this approach.
5. Current information from Brunswick Brokerage, Moscow, early July 1997. The market capitalization of the 200 companies actively traded on the Moscow stock market was assessed at $20.8 billion in April 1996 (*Russian Economic Trends* 1996, p. 32).
6. For a similar argument at a general level, see Maravall (1994, pp. 17–31) and Geddes (1994, pp. 104–118).
7. An initial discussion of this is found in Åslund, Boone, and Johnson (1996, pp. 273–288).

References

Åslund, Anders. 1995. *How Russia Became a Market Economy.* Washington, D.C.: Brookings.

———. 1996. "Reform vs. 'Rent-Seeking' in Russia's Economic Transformation." *Transition* 26: 12–16.

Åslund, Anders, Peter Boone, and Simon Johnson. 1996. "How to Stabilize: Lessons from Post-Communist Countries." *Brookings Papers on Economic Activity* 1: 217–291.

Aven, Petr O. 1994. "Problems in Foreign Trade Regulation in the Russian Economic Reform." In *Economic Transformation in Russia*, Anders Åslund, ed. London: Pinter, p. 84.

Balcerowicz, Leszek. 1994. "Understanding Postcommunist Transitions." *Journal of Democracy* 5(4): 75–89.

Blasi, Joseph R., Maya Kroumova, and Douglas Kruse. 1997. *Kremlin Capitalism: Privatizing the Russian Economy.* Ithaca, New York: Cornell University Press.

Boycko, Maxim, Andrei Shleifer, and Robert Vishny. 1995. *Privatizing Russia.* Cambridge, Massachusetts: MIT Press.

Brown, Annette N., Barry Ickes, and Randi Ryterman. 1994. "The Myth of Monopoly: A New View of Industrial Structure in Russia." World Bank Policy Research Working Paper No. 1331, World Bank, Washington, D.C., August.

Dmitriev, M.S., M. Yu Matovnikov, L.V. Mikhailov, L.I. Sycheve, E.V. Timofeev, and A. Warner. 1996. *Rossiiskie banki nakanune finansovoi stabilizatsii.* St. Petersburg: Norma.

Geddes, Barbara. 1994. "Challenging the Conventional Wisdom." *Journal of Democracy* 5(4): 104–118.

Goldman, Marshall I. 1994. *Lost Opportunity: Why Economic Reforms in Russia Have Not Worked.* New York: Norton.

Goskomstat. 1994. *Sotsialina-ekonomicheskoe polozhenie Rossii 1993g.*, Moscow: Goskomstat.

Granville, Brigitte. 1995. *The Success of Russian Economic Reform.* London: Royal Institute of International Affairs.

Hellman, Joel. 1998. "Winners Take All: The Politics of Partial Reform in Postcommunist Transitions." *World Politics* 50(January): 203–234.

International Monetary Fund. 1993. *Economic Review: Russian Federation.* Washington, D.C.

Kaufmann, Daniel, and Paul Siegelbaum. 1996. "Privatization and Corruption in Transition Economies." *Journal of International Affairs* 50(2): 419–458.

Kornai, János. 1992. *The Socialist System: The Political Economy of Communism.* Princeton: Princeton University Press.

Layard, Richard, and Andrea Richter. 1994. "Who Gains and Who Loses from Russian Credit Expansion?" *Communist Economies and Economic Transformation* 6(16): 459–471.

Lipton, David, and Jeffrey D. Sachs. 1990. "Creating a Market in Eastern Europe: The Case of Poland." *Brookings Papers on Economic Activity* 1: 75–147.

Maravall, Jose Maria. 1994. "The Myth of Authoritarian Advantage." *Journal of Democracy* 5(4): 17–31.

Nelson, Lynn D., and Irina Y. Kuzes. 1995. *Radical Reform in Yeltsin's Russia: Political, Economic, and Social Dimensions.* Armonk, New York: M.E. Sharpe.

Olson, Mancur. 1971. *The Logic of Collective Action: Public Goods and the Theory of Groups.* Second ed. Cambridge, Massachusetts: Harvard University Press.

Russian Economic Trends. 1996. Monthly Update, July 16. Moscow: Russian European Centre for Economic Policy. See http://cep.lse.ac.uk/datalib/ret.

Shleifer, Andrei, and Robert W. Vishny. 1993. "Corruption." *Quarterly Journal of Economics* 108(3): 599–617.

World Bank. 1996. *World Development Report 1996: From Plan to Market.* Oxford: Oxford University Press.

4 China's Unfinished Economic Transition

Nicholas R. Lardy
The Brookings Institution

The hallmark of China's approach to economic reform is gradualism. China's reformers, in effect, have eschewed the conventional wisdom that successful economic transitions are built on the basis of rapid privatization of state-owned firms, overnight price reform, and a quick dismantling of trade barriers. Although a variety of new forms of ownership have flourished in China, de facto privatization of small state-owned firms did not get underway until the mid 1990s, and few, if any, medium and large state-owned firms have been privatized. Relative prices in China for the most part have converged to world levels, but this process was extremely gradual. Opening the economy to foreign trade was similarly gradual and was a key part of the process by which relative domestic prices have converged to world levels. Moreover, foreign trade liberalization is far from complete, as China maintains a trade system with substantial protection for many industries.

Paradoxically, China's economic performance, by almost all measures, has been superior to that in other transition economies. In contrast to a period of sharply declining output in several of the states of Eastern Europe and the former Soviet Union, China's gradual reform generated record rates of economic growth from the outset. From 1978 through 1995, real output increased at an average annual rate of 8 percent. Unlike the transition in Russia, where inflation accelerated dramatically, China has held average annual inflation to a single-digit level, despite two sharp upward spikes, since economic reform began in the late 1970s. Moreover, economic growth in China has been broadly shared among all regions and segments of society. The precipitous decline in poverty in the first seven years of economic reform was especially dramatic. By contrast, in Russia, the combination of a disintegrating social safety net and declining real output has inflicted sharply lower living standards on large segments of the population, even as a small class of *nouveau riche* Russians enjoy ostentatious lifestyles. Finally, China's gradual reforms facilitated its progress toward integration into the world economy. By the mid 1990s, China's share of world trade had quintupled relative to the pre-reform period, and it regularly was the recipient of more foreign direct investment than any other transition or developing country. Moreover, it was the first transition economy to be awarded an investment-grade rating for its sovereign debt in international capital markets, and it has raised far more capital in these markets than any other transition economy.

THE SUSTAINABILITY OF CHINA'S STRATEGY

Despite these apparent successes, I believe that China's current economic policy mix is unsustainable and that the completion of China's economic transition will require a more accelerated reform strategy. Three trends are particularly worrisome. First, state-owned enterprises are becoming ever more indebted, particularly to banks. These firms increasingly borrow not only to finance the purchase of new equipment or other productive assets, but also to buy inputs used in production, to pay their wage bills, to provide a broad range of social services to their workers, and, in some cases, even to meet their pension and tax obligations. In short, on average they are not able to cover their total costs with the income they receive from the sales of their products.

Second, state-owned banks and other financial institutions are extending loans at what appears to be a pace that will not be economically sustainable. Loans outstanding relative to gross domestic product (GDP) have doubled since reform began in 1978. By year-end 1997, loans outstanding were equal to total output. Most of these loans from banks and other financial institutions have been extended to state-owned enterprises, and a large and rising share is nonperforming, meaning that the borrowers are no longer repaying principal or even interest on their loans. As a result, the profitability of the banks, as measured by return on assets, has fallen by five-sixths since the mid 1980s. Given the modest amount of their own capital, their tiny loan-loss reserves, and nonperforming loans acknowledged to be equal to fully one-fourth of their loan portfolios, by Western accounting standards several of China's major state-owned banks already are insolvent. Since households continue to add enormous amounts of funds to their savings accounts, these banks remain liquid and a financial crisis has been avoided. However, this cannot continue in the long run.

Third, government tax revenues declined by two-thirds relative to output between 1978 and 1995. At the beginning of reform, taxes and other government revenues were equal to a third of the nation's output, a level well above the average of other transition economies. By 1995, revenues had fallen to about 10 percent, a level quite low in comparison with both other transition economies and emerging markets. As a result, during the reform era the state increasingly has been unable to finance normal government expenditures from the budget. Although the official budget deficit has been modest and in recent years financed entirely through the sale of treasury bonds, the broader public sector nonfinancial deficit in the mid 1990s has been running at an unsustainable level of over 10 percent of gross domestic output for almost a decade. That deficit reflects the increased borrowing demand of state-owned industrial and commercial firms, a portion of which represents social and other expenditures that should be financed through the state budget.

In short, the strategy of gradualism of the Deng Xiaoping era appears to be economically unsustainable. Moreover, since the three trends described are closely interrelated, a strategy of focusing sequentially on the problems of banking, state-owned enterprises, and taxes is not likely to be effective. The banks cannot operate on fully commercial terms until the behavior of their principal borrowers fundamentally changes. However, many potentially profitable enterprises will find it difficult to improve their financial performance and to deal with banks on a normal commercial basis until the state relieves them of the obligation of providing a broad range of social services and of employing more workers than economically are necessary. The government will not be able to finance either these social expenditures or the needed recapitalization of the banking system from the budget until a fundamental reform of tax policy and tax administration increases government revenues relative to output. Thus, the key to reform in the future is likely to be a strategy that addresses all three of the underlying problems simultaneously.

REFORM OF THE BANKING SYSTEM

The creation of a modern banking system is essential to improving the efficiency with which capital is allocated and to sustaining rapid economic growth in all transition economies. Banking reform in all transition economies must be based on the rehabilitation of existing banks, on the entry of new banks, or on some combination. China's approach to date emphasizes rehabilitation but also includes the establishment of some new banks and other new financial institutions. This is an appropriate mix given China's unusually high ratio of bank deposits to GDP. Relying primarily on new institutions may be a viable strategy in Russia and in the other newly independent states, where high inflation in the early 1990s so reduced the value of savings deposits that the ratio of deposits to GDP in 1994 was only one-sixth that in China. Relying largely on new institutions in China would inevitably mean the collapse of existing banks, wiping out most of the value of household savings deposits, which at year-end 1997 were RMB 4.6 trillion, the equivalent of well over one-half of GDP. That could create a financial crisis.

The rehabilitation of existing banks depends critically on their recapitalization. There is only one other alternative—a default on household liabilities. This was feasible in Russia both because the value of household deposits in the banking system was quite low, about 10 percent of GDP, and because Russia had already entered the post-communist era. The mechanism through which household savings were lost was several years of hyperinflation that effectively eliminated the purchasing power of funds tied up in bank deposits on which very low rates of interest were paid. However, the default on the much larger volume of household savings in China, whether explicit through a collapse of the banking system or implicit through the inflation tax, would likely lead to a political crisis. Thus, China's leadership is likely to eschew defaulting on liabilities to households and make good on its existing implicit guarantee of the value of all household deposits in the banking system. That approach requires a write-off of bad debt and a recapitalization of the banks.

One approach is the gradual recapitalization of banks through reinvestment of their profits. The World Bank's 1996 *World Development Report*, which focused on the problems of transition economies, is skeptical of the long-term efficacy of using tax revenues to recapitalize banks in transition economies. This view is based in part on the early Hungarian transition experience, in which some banks were recapitalized as many as five times. The *World Development Report* favors policies that promote self-help for banks, to encourage them to build up their capital base and to grow out of their bad-debt problems.

While this strategy may have merit in other transition economies, it is much less feasible for China. The magnitude of nonperforming loans, and thus the size of the required recapitalization, are so large that the incremental rebuilding of capital through the reinvestment of profits does not appear viable. The gradual approach, sometimes called a flow solution, is feasible in the most mild cases of banking distress, where capital adequacy of problem banks, while low, is still positive. As noted, several of China's major state-owned banks are effectively insolvent; that is, the value of their liabilities exceeds the value of their assets. Moreover, the reported level of profitability of these banks has fallen to quite low levels, and, according to realistic accounting principles, is almost certainly negative. In short, there are no real profits to be added to bank capital.

The bottom line is that China's best option is probably to follow the course pursued by several transition economies in Eastern Europe: to recapitalize the banks by injecting government bonds into these institutions in an amount equal to the value of the write-offs that must be taken of the nonperforming loans. Since loans outstanding now are fully equal to China's GDP, the fiscal cost of this approach will be high. For example, if the bad loans that ultimately need to be written off total one-fourth of banks' loan portfolios and the real interest rate on government bonds is 6 percent, the annual interest the government would have to pay on the bonds issued would be equal to 1.5 percent of GDP. That would absorb about one-eighth of the current level of combined government expenditures at the central, provincial, and local levels. Since China's existing stock of government debt is quite low, for some period of time much of the interest cost could be financed by the sale of additional bonds to the public, rather than by cutting other expenditures. Ultimately, financing the recapitalization of the banks will require increased tax revenues relative to output of the economy, reversing the long-term decline.

If China fails to complete the transformation of its banking system, the consequences are predictable. The intermediation of funds between savers and investors by banks likely would continue to be marked by the inefficiencies already evident. As the contributions to economic growth of various one-time factors wind down, one would expect the rate of growth of the economy to slow. That trend would be reinforced by the physical constraints to growth that are increasingly evident in China: environmental deterioration, the challenge of sustaining adequate gains in agricultural output, and infrastructure shortages. Unless resources are used more efficiently in industry and commerce, it is difficult to foresee how China could overcome these physical limitations. An inefficient banking system also would impede the development of stock and bond markets; as per-capita output rises and appropriate regulatory structures are developed, these markets normally come to play an important supplementary role in the allocation of resources. The continued fragility of the banking system would limit the ability of the People's Bank, through the more active use of interest rate policy, to dampen the marked fluctuations in economic activity that have characterized the reform era. Ultimately, the failure to transform the banking system could undermine the high rate of household savings that has provided most of the fuel for China's strong economic growth.

The international consequences of China's failure to complete the transformation of its banking system also are predictable. A sound banking system is a prerequisite for moving to convertibility on capital account transactions. This factor underlies the reluctance of government officials to declare an unduly optimistic target date for achieving full convertibility of the domestic currency. Until China's banking system has been restructured and placed on a sound financial foundation, the People's Bank will almost certainly continue to require foreign financial institutions to operate under the many severe restrictions that already exist. Consequently, the expectation of the international community that China will provide national treatment[1] of foreign banks and nonbank financial institutions will not be met. This expectation is likely to be reflected in any protocol governing China's accession to the World Trade Organization.

CONCLUSION

By many measures, China's economic transition looks relatively good. However, gradualism has had a significant downside that becomes apparent once one looks at the economy, particularly the financial system, in greater depth. The cost of deferring industrial restructuring has been high. Real resources have continued to flow into enterprises that will not be viable in a market economy. These resource movements have been intermediated through the banking system, which relies almost entirely on household savings as the source of its funds. Thus, sustaining money-losing state-owned enterprises has involved the accumulation of huge liabilities to households. In addition, since the users of borrowed funds in many cases are no longer able to repay principal or even to pay interest on their loans, the liabilities of banks to households are no longer backed by real assets. This creates the potential for a domestic banking crisis that would disrupt the flow of credit and the payments system, leading to a major recession. The failure of major banks also could have long-term negative implications for the high rate of household savings, which has become the principal source of growth in the reform era.

Avoiding a financial meltdown will entail the substantial economic costs associated with recapitalization and commercialization of the banking system, with an accelerated program of privatization and restructuring of state-owned firms, and with a fiscal reform that raises the tax share of GDP. Although these changes probably would curtail the rate of economic growth somewhat in the short run, they would be highly desirable in the long run since they would help the emergence of a more efficient system of financial intermediation and a more productive manufacturing sector. Avoiding a financial meltdown also will entail substantial short-term social and political costs. Shutting down large numbers of inefficient, money-losing state-owned enterprises is a prerequisite to creating an efficient, modern banking system. Banks will not be able to operate on commercial principles if they are required to continue to prop up inefficient firms with an ever-growing volume of loans. This will lead to reduced incomes for a significant portion of China's population, at least on a transitory basis. Already-high rates of unemployment are likely to rise further before the efficiency gains of accelerated reform lead to an improved allocation of resources and increased rates of job creation. Thus, the next stage of reform carries with it unprecedented potential for social unrest.

NOTE

1. I.e., that foreign banks will be allowed to provide the same range of services to their customers as domestic banks do.

5 The Transition Is Not Over, but Note the Merits of the Central European Model

Jan Švejnar
William Davidson Institute and *University of Michigan*

I define economic transition as a process that is completed when two conditions hold:

a) central planning is abolished and no longer serves as the allocational and distributional mechanism in the economy, and

b) central planning and direct government intervention is replaced by an efficiently functioning market system. The term "efficiently functioning market system" is, of course, key and needs further definition. I take it to mean that the transition economies generate relatively rapid and sustainable rates of economic growth and become compatible with advanced market economies in the sense that neither side requires major protection through subsidies or barriers against trade, capital flows, and labor mobility.

The first condition has been met in a number of economies, including those that are doing relatively well (e.g., Hungary, Poland, and Slovenia), as well as those whose economic performance has been poor (e.g., Russia and Ukraine). It must also be noted that countries such as Slovenia and Croatia have been displaying many of the transition features, but their starting point was a labor-managed system with social ownership and substantial government intervention. The first condition may hence be regarded as being a necessary one for the transition to proceed but not a sufficient one for the transition to be completed.

The second condition defines the end of the transition process as being the state of an advanced market economy. No transition economy has so far satisfied this condition, and the study of how emerging market economies become mature market economies is in fact the study of the fulfillment of this second condition.

Given my definition, it is not surprising that I have questioned declarations such as that of the Czech prime minister in 1995, when he stated that the transition was accomplished, with the remaining tasks being secondary and akin to fine-tuning in the Western economies.

Indeed, 1995 was a year for euphoria. As may be seen from Table 1 (on p. 93), the Czech Republic and the other Central European economies[1] emerged from one of the most severe depressions experienced any where in Europe in the twentieth century. With the exception of Hungary, economic growth was rapid across the region, and in most countries the rate of growth was accelerating. Inflation, which at the start of the 1990s reached the hyper zone in a number of Central European economies, was curtailed (Table 2). In some countries (e.g., the Czech and Slovak republics and Slovenia), the rate of inflation dipped into single digits, and in all countries in Central Europe it was below 40 percent. Unemployment, which appeared in most Central European countries in 1990 and reached a double-digit rate in all except the Czech Republic by 1992, started to show a declining tendency in 1995 (Table 3). Slovenia as well as the Czech and Slovak republics were running balanced budgets, while the other economies were making serious strides toward reducing their budget deficits (Table 4). Foreign direct investment, while modest compared to earlier expectations, was showing signs of acceleration (Table 5). The Czech Republic, Hungary, and Slovakia obtained sovereign debt ratings by Standard & Poor's, and the other countries were on their way to being rated (Table 6).

The "Central European model" of transition from Soviet-style central planning seemed to be working and doing much better than the "Russian and Newly Independent States (NIS) model" in the former Soviet Union. Taking Russia and Ukraine as examples of the latter model, we see that these countries experienced a much longer period of deep economic decline (Table 1) and only recently started to recover.[2] Russia and Ukraine also suffered from a longer spell of high inflation (Table 2) and recorded lower unemployment rates (especially Ukraine), as restructuring of firms proceeded at a slower pace, and lowering (late payment) of wages and relying on shorter hours were preferred to layoffs as a form of labor force adjustment (Table 3). As may be seen from Table 4, the prolonged inflationary period had an underpinning in significant budget deficits in the first half of the 1990s. Both Russia and Ukraine attracted only modest amounts of foreign direct investment (Table 5), and it was not until 1996 that Russia (but not Ukraine) obtained a rating (BB-) from Standard & Poor's (Table 6).

China and Vietnam represent the third model of transition. This "Asian model" has appeared very attractive from a number of standpoints. It has been characterized by very rapid economic growth, which in the 1990s exceeded 10 percent in China and hovered around 9 percent in Vietnam (Table 1). Moreover, China's period of rapid economic growth has lasted two full decades. Inflation has fluctuated widely in both countries, but for most of the 1990s the rate of inflation was well below 20 percent (Table 2). Unemployment is hard to measure in these highly agrarian economies, but until recently urban unemployment (based on official registry data) was relatively limited (Table 3).[3] China has also kept its budget deficit under control, and Vietnam has gradually brought its sizable deficit down (Table 4). Finally, China has been relatively successful in attracting foreign direct investment (Table 5), and it secured sovereign debt rating as early as 1993 (Table 6).

Using a number of performance indicators, such as the ones in Tables 1–5, the Asian model appears to have produced the best results, followed by the Central European model. The Russian-NIS model has usually been seen as the least successful. The picture changed a bit in 1996–1997, as the economic performance of some Central European countries deteriorated. Thus, the Czech Republic saw a slowdown in economic growth, and in the Balkans, Bulgaria and Romania experienced a deceleration that turned into decline (Table 1). In the Czech Republic, the early diagnosis suggests that the country did not succeed in adequately restructuring its firms and in establishing a well-functioning legal and regulatory system. Bulgaria and Romania have suffered from the same problem, coupled with a loss of macroeconomic control (Tables 2 and 4). At the same time, in 1997, there were signs that Russia experienced its first period of economic growth and that the rate of economic decline was decelerating in Ukraine. Overall, while the rate of growth of gross domestic product (GDP) slowed in Central and Eastern Europe (including the Balkans and the Baltic states) from over 5 percent in 1995 to about 3 percent in 1997, the Commonwealth of Independent States (CIS) turned a 1 percent decline into a 1 percent rate of growth during the same period. The 1998 crisis showed that the Russian and CIS model was fragile.

I will review the principal aspects of the transformation in Central Europe and contrast these features with those of the transition economies in the other models. Then I will discuss the challenges faced by Central Europe if it is to complete its economic transition.

THE PRINCIPAL ASPECTS OF CENTRAL EUROPEAN TRANSITION

Some outcomes have been relatively systematic, while others have varied across the Central European countries. The systematic developments—those that are similar across countries—are the transformation of these economies from centrally planned or government-guided, labor-managed economies to essentially market economies; relatively successful macroeconomic stabilization (exemplified by the countries' ability to contain initial inflationary pressures); opening up to world trade and reorienting trade from East to West; the rapid creation of a large number of small- and medium-sized enterprises; significant reduction in state subsidies to firms together with the creation of a substantial social safety net; and the development of laws, institutions, and practices conducive to the functioning of labor, capital, and goods markets.

Outcomes that have varied across these countries include the extent of privatization and restructuring of state enterprises; the rates of unemployment and duration of unemployment spells; the ability to contain budget deficits and foreign indebtedness; and the perceived effectiveness of reforms as measured by the rate of domestic investment, inflow of foreign direct investment, foreign trade performance, and rate of economic growth.

The Systematic Developments

The most notable outcome of the first eight years of the transition in Central Europe is that these economies have undergone a virtually complete transformation from disintegrating central planning (or centralized labor-management) into an imperfect but vibrant market system. Broadly speaking, these economies now operate on market principles. Most prices are free and reflect relative scarcities of resources. The economies are open to international trade and are composed of a dynamic and rapidly growing sector of new private firms, together with a heterogeneous but generally shrinking sector of the old (in most countries, former) state enterprises. In this respect, the Central European economies resemble China, where the township and village enterprises (TVEs), operating under relatively hard budget constraints and market principles, have also provided a major impetus for economic development. The picture has been quite different in Russia and in many of the newly independent states, where market forces are still weak and the impact of new firms is limited.

Eager to dismantle the Council for Mutual Economic Assistance (CMEA) trading system that existed within the Soviet bloc and faced with a collapsing Soviet market, the Central European economies have dramatically reoriented their trade (see, for example, Brabant 1993). While all of them traded for decades primarily within the CMEA, by 1993–1994 the European Community replaced the ex-CMEA region as their principal trading partner. This achievement is notable for two reasons: 1) few observers had expected these countries to be able to penetrate substantially the advanced Western markets, and virtually no one had expected them to do so in such a short time interval, and 2) the reorientation was carried out to a large extent by state enterprises before any privatization took place. Major currency devaluations, reductions of subsidies to firms, and the opening of trade have been the factors driving the transformation in this area. In their ability to export manufactured goods, the Central European countries again more resemble China than the CIS countries, which, except for export of raw materials, have remained relatively self-contained. In contrast to China, the Central European countries have also opened up much more to imports and capital flows.

While undertaking bold transformation measures, the Central European countries have been quick to provide a relatively complete and generous social safety net. Unemployment benefits were originally set at high levels and remain adequate even after rounds of reductions in the midst of reforms. A broadly defined system, providing welfare, pension, and health care benefits, was also put in place. The system has so far enabled policymakers in Central Europe to prevent the emergence of major income inequality and poverty, unlike the situation in Russia (see Garner and Terrell 1998). In China, most of the economy has not been covered by a central social safety net. The net exists in the case of state-owned firms, but the government is currently moving to reduce its fiscal obligations toward workers in these enterprises.

Diverse Outcomes

Privatization of state enterprises has proceeded very unevenly across the Central European economies. In the Czech and Slovak republics, for example, most state-owned enterprises (SOEs) have been mass-privatized, but restructuring and productivity growth have been slow. In contrast, Poland, Hungary, and Slovenia initially placed less emphasis on privatizing the state-owned firms, but unit labor cost, expressed in German marks, has been rising more slowly in these economies than in the Czech and Slovak republics. In fact, in the first half of the 1990s, the emphasis in Poland and Slovenia shifted from privatization to commercialization of state or socially owned enterprises. Only in the last two years has there been a significant move in these economies to privatize state or socially owned firms. Hungary has pursued a persistent policy of individual sales of firms and has succeeded in selling a significant share of the economy over the last eight years. In this aspect of the transition process, Russia resembles more the Czech and Slovak republics in that it mass-privatized. The process and the recipients of property have differed, but in both cases the resulting corporate governance has been taking time to be organized. China and Vietnam more resemble Poland and Slovenia, in that until recently they focused less on privatization of SOEs and more on other aspects of the transition.

Firms in all of the Central European countries decreased employment as they experienced falling demand for their output in the early 1990s. The amount of labor force adjustment differed, however, across the individual countries. Firms in Hungary, for example, adjusted employment more than those in the Czech Republic. Using large enterprise-level data sets with annual observations from the pretransition and transition period, Basu, Estrin, and Švejnar (1995a, 1995b) in fact show that the extent of pretransition "marketization" of the economy is correlated with the extent of employment adjustment in the early phase of the transition. In particular, in 1989 and 1990, Czech and Slovak firms behaved in accordance with a stereotype of a labor-hoarding firm in a planned economy—not being forced to adjust employment in response to changes in output and wages. The Polish firms conformed to the stereotype of operating in a semimarket economy by showing moderate sensitivity of employment to output and wages. Estimates for later years indicate that all three economies converged to higher elasticities, thus displaying behavior similar to that observed in Western market economies. In contrast, data from Russian industrial firms fail to show any significant elasticity of labor demand to wages as late as 1993–1994.

The levels of investment declined in Central Europe during the first phase of the transition in the early 1990s, but by the mid 1990s they began to improve. In fact, it appears that by the mid 1990s, gross investment returned to relatively high levels (around 30 percent of GDP) in the Czech and Slovak republics and to respectable levels (over 20 percent of GDP) in Poland and Hungary. The Czech and Slovak levels are comparable to those in China and Vietnam, while the levels in Poland and Hungary resemble those observed in Western Europe. In contrast, according to data from the European Bank for Reconstruction and Development (EBRD), investment continued to decline at a rapid pace in Russia through the mid 1990s.

At about 70 percent and 40 percent, respectively, Hungary and Poland registered the highest foreign debt/GNP ratios in the region in the early to mid 1990s. In contrast, Slovenia's ratio was about 5 percent, and the Czech Republic's was below 25 percent. The different burdens of indebtedness influenced the approach that the individual countries adopted toward carrying out the transformation to a market economy. Hungary, having been saddled with the highest foreign debt, has, for instance, decided to privatize by selling firms individually to foreign and domestic bidders, while the Czech Republic gave out substantial stakes in firms to citizens at large through the voucher privatization method.

Although the Central European countries all succeeded in reorienting trade from Eastern to Western partners, their exchange rate policies and the resulting foreign trade performances have been diverse. For example, while Poland and Hungary repeatedly devalued their currencies and eventually adopted a crawling peg system as their exchange rate policy, the Czechs and Slovaks followed the approach of a fixed exchange rate until 1997 and 1998, respectively. This policy resulted in an overvaluation of the Czech and Slovak currencies relative to those of Poland and Hungary. Consequently, while Poland and to a lesser extent Hungary registered solid growth of exports in the mid 1990s, the Czech and Slovak republics have been experiencing slower export growth and increasingly severe balance-of-trade and payments deficits. The Czechs were forced to abandon the fixed exchange rate in 1997, and the Slovaks in 1998. The policy of overvalued exchange rates, in my view, explains a significant part (though not all) of the poorer economic performance of the Czech Republic relative to that of other Central European countries in 1996, 1997, and 1998.

THE CHALLENGES AHEAD

The developments to date point to a number of challenges that the Central European economies must meet if they are to improve their efficiency, raise their living standards, and thus complete their transition to well-functioning and relatively advanced market economies. The foremost challenge is how to generate high and sustained rates of economic growth. This challenge has several underpinnings. The principal aspect is the political one, namely, that economic growth with widely reaching benefits is a prerequisite for maintaining momentum in the transition. Since the early post-revolutionary euphoria has by now evaporated, it is increasingly difficult for politicians to secure consensus for major restructuring (be it at the level of firms, banks, or the pension and health system). Of course, there is a chicken-and-egg problem here: cooperation of the people is needed for restructuring and growth, but the benefits of growth are needed for inducing cooperation. In view of the slowdown in economic growth in the region over the last three years, the question is whether the Central European countries will be able to maintain the momentum to complete the transition.

Put in more quantitative terms, the fundamental question is whether the Central European economies can generate long-term growth of GDP of 7 percent or more. With GDP per capita in Central Europe at 25–40 percent of the Western European average, high growth rates will have to be achieved and sustained if these countries are to start closing the relative productivity and income gap with Western Europe and the OECD countries in general. This challenge is truly formidable. The following tasks, in my view, constitute the building blocks for meeting this challenge.

A high rate of efficiently placed investment is a prerequisite for economic growth in the region. In view of past developments, this requirement is still a major hurdle for the Central European economies. As the transformation to a market economy unfolded, it was expected that market forces would induce a dramatic improvement in the efficiency of investment and that the key problem would be the availability of capital embodying modern technology. It turns out that, while the availability of capital clearly became a major concern for many firms, poor credit allocation by many banks has meant that the efficiency of capital allocation did not increase as much as was anticipated.

The transition was hence expected to result in a partial reversal of the previous situation, in which the rates of investment were high but the efficiency of capital allocation was poor.[4] The decade of the 1980s was marked by a fall in the rate of investment in many Central and Eastern European economies, together with the acceleration of technical progress in the West and the Western embargo on exports of high technology to the Soviet bloc. These factors brought about the worsening of the relative technological position of the Central and Eastern European economies. With the notable exception of Slovenia, these countries entered the transition facing an acute need to spur investment embodying modern technology. So far they have succeeded only in part, primarily in instances where there have been major Western investments.

A key problem in this context has been the limited inflow of foreign direct investment in all Central European countries except Hungary. While the situation appears to be changing, the inflow over the first eight years of the transition has been small in comparison to the annual inflows of foreign direct investment in the (until recently) rapidly growing East Asian economies. One problem is that, in an attempt to reduce budgetary deficits and to establish adequate social safety nets, most transitional economies have imposed high corporate taxes, which put a brake on foreign, as well as domestic, investment. Another problem is that Western investors have been wary of many Central and Eastern European economies. Perceived uncertainty has been high, deriving in part from unclear property rights and nontransparent regulation of the financial sector in some economies. The clear lesson is that attracting foreign direct investment is a long and arduous process.

On the domestic front, the capital market has been developing only slowly as an effective source of investment funds. The banking sector is still highly concentrated, often significantly state-owned and inefficient, and facing limited foreign competition. Interest rates on loans have been high as banks have been allowed to keep a sizable spread between deposit and lending rates in order to create reserves. Moreover, central banks have often pursued high-interest-rate policies in order to prevent capital flight. The problem has been especially acute for export-oriented firms in countries maintaining overvalued exchange rates. These firms have faced moderate Western inflation in the product market and relatively high domestic interest rate costs.

High interest rates have also slowed the development of small- and medium-sized firms. Moreover, after an initial period of easy lending to small private-sector firms, banks have in recent years restricted lending to and set high collateral requirements for small businesses. Given the key role that this sector has played in the transformation so far, it is clear that future overall business performance will be jeopardized if this part of the economy becomes significantly handicapped.

The situation of loan shortages is partly brought about by asymmetric information between the banks and entrepreneurs. The banks often report that they have funds but cannot find good projects, while entrepreneurs claim that they are not able to get financing for projects with high expected returns. The problem is related to the fact that commercial banks in Central Europe have not had an adequate number of well-trained and experienced loan officers and that they have generally suffered from inefficient operations. These shortcomings result in a limited ability of the banks to appraise and monitor projects. Still, lending funds to enterprises whose liquidation value may be very low requires that the banks be able to track and control the operation. If this condition cannot be fulfilled because the banks cannot obtain reliable information, the banks will prefer not to lend or will require very high collateral. Another frequently cited reason for a lack of lending to small- and medium-sized firms is the established relationship between banks and large firms and corruption. This is hard to substantiate, but the fact that the quality of loan portfolios of a number of banks in the region has severely deteriorated after they were restructured in the early 1990s means that there has been a problem with the efficiency of the banking sector during the transition.

The allocative role of the stock markets has so far been minimal. Stock markets have been successfully established in most Central European countries, but their trading volumes have been low. Moreover, in some countries, transactions often take place outside the stock markets, thus further reducing their effectiveness.

With external funds being limited, firms have naturally turned to internal financing. Yet, with profits often falling, many enterprises have been unable to raise much investment capital internally in the first few years of the transition. The well-performing ones have increasingly done so, and the imposition of hard budget constraints, price liberalization, and opening up to the world have improved allocation of resources. There are also signs that Western banks have been increasing direct lending to successful businesses in the region.

The second building block for meeting the fundamental challenge of growth is human capital development. One feature that distinguishes the Central European economies from those of many developing countries is the relatively high level of general, as well as specific, education (Boeri and Keese 1992). Since these countries are also relatively poor in natural resources, investment in human capital is strategically important for their economic progress. Nevertheless, investment in education as well as in research and development (R&D) has been given relatively low priority during the transition. As a result, there has been limited R&D and a significant brain drain in these nations.

The third building block consists of smoothly functioning labor markets and social safety nets. With the notable exception of the Czech Republic, a major challenge for the Central European countries in the 1990s has been unemployment. The problem has been addressed by putting into place adequate social safety nets and by pursuing active labor market policies, such as training of the unemployed. Unfortunately, active micropolicies alone are unlikely to dramatically improve labor market efficiency and to substantially reduce unemployment. For example, investing in greater labor mobility across districts would have little effect on unemployment, because the number of jobless within each district greatly exceeds the number of vacancies, both in general and within each educational category (Munich, Švejnar, and Terrell 1995). Macroeconomic policies and, more generally, those that stimulate economic growth are the more promising solution to the unemployment problem.

The task of reducing unemployment has been complicated by the fact that the provision of social safety nets has been taxing, especially in Hungary and to a lesser extent in Poland, where foreign indebtedness and budget deficits have been major problems. Containing public expenditures will clearly be important but difficult in the face of high unemployment and dissatisfaction with the social cost of transition.

A particularly challenging task in this context is the reduction in the cost of retirement benefits. In this respect, the Central European countries are significantly worse off than either Russia or China, where the burden of retirement benefits is less pronounced. The Central European countries entered the transition period with publicly funded pension systems, almost universal coverage of the population, low retirement ages (on average 60 for men and 55 for women), high and growing dependency ratios, large expenditure and contribution levels, high statutory replacement rates (retirement benefits replace a high proportion of the individual's wages), and a perverse redistribution of benefits. The result of the high dependency ratio is that the system has been very costly and yet offers relatively low benefits (because a large proportion of the population gets retirement benefits, the level of benefits is low). With an aging population and a pay-as-you-go system, the tax burden becomes increasingly heavy. Several countries have already moved to raise the retirement age and to supplement the public retirement system with voluntary private schemes; these are clearly steps in the right direction, but more will need to be done. Raising the retirement age is needed on fiscal as well as on efficiency grounds, although the short-term effect may be an upturn in the already high unemployment rates. Lowering the average wage replacement rate to the level of OECD countries would be desirable, especially if part of the benefits of this restructuring could be channeled into a newly established system of private (supplementary) savings for retirement. Shifting the public system to a broader and less distorting tax base than payroll is also desirable on efficiency and distributional grounds.

A major challenge lies in establishing effective corporate governance, which is a fourth building block for growth. The power of managers and workers (insiders) is often significant, and neither government nor new private owners provide effective control in many firms. The Polish government, for example, yielded significant control rights to workers and managers already in the 1980s and thus entered the transition with limited powers over enterprises. In contrast, the Czech and Slovak governments kept tight reins during the mass privatization process, but the new dispersed owners or their investment fund representatives have not exercised effective control over management in many privatized firms. The problem is all the more serious because the Central European economies still suffer from a shortage of managerial skills. Managers of (former) state-owned enterprises tend to underestimate the importance of key activities such as quality improvement, marketing, and accounting and audit.

In countries such as the Czech Republic and Slovakia, a conflict of interest has also developed between the banks and the investment privatization funds. With some of the largest funds being owned by the large commercial banks, a bank's desire to initiate bankruptcy of firms may go counter to the interest of the investment fund holding shares of these firms. It is also difficult because the legal system and its enforcement is inadequate. The situation may be serious enough to account in part for the lower volume of bankruptcies in Slovakia and the Czech Republic relative to, for example, Hungary and Poland.

The European Union (EU) is the obvious destination for the Central European countries and thus is an important component of their future growth. Accession negotiations have been under way for several years, and the economic phenomena discussed in this paper are important for the timing of joining. Indeed, much of the economic restructuring observed in these countries is influenced by EU policies, such as the requirement that Central European firms be competitive with their EU counterparts as a precondition to entry into the Union.

A problematic aspect of the relationship between Central and Western Europe is the fact that the "safeguard restrictions" and antidumping procedures used by EU members represent a hindrance to exports from and growth in Central Europe. Studies indicate that the economic impact of exports from Central Europe to the EU is very limited, albeit focused in a few areas. The challenge for the Central European economies is to find freer access to EU markets, to use this access to complete restructuring, and eventually to become EU members.

CONCLUDING OBSERVATIONS

In the early and mid 1990s, the countries of Central Europe carried out the first phase of a historically unprecedented transformation of their centrally planned economies. Despite many remaining imperfections, these countries now have functioning market economies. They have to overcome major structural problems and to meet the lofty expectations of their peoples. Above all, they face the daunting task of generating the resources and governance structures needed to launch high and sustained rates of economic growth that will improve their efficiency, living standards, and chances of gaining EU membership. In many respects, this challenge, which is more subtle than the earlier elimination of the planning mechanism and the introduction of the basic building blocks of a market system, is the more difficult part of the transition process.

NOTES

1. There is no strict definition of "Central Europe." In this article, I will focus on the Czech Republic, Hungary, Poland, Slovakia, and Slovenia (the so-called Visegrad countries).
2. The numbers reported in Table 1 are official estimates. With underreporting of economic activity apparently being serious, the official figures may overestimate the degree of economic decline. A similar problem of biased reporting exists in Central Europe. The question is whether the problem was more intense in Russia and Ukraine.
3. Recently, there have been indications that local unemployment has risen in a number of northern areas of China.
4. Edward Gierek's big push to import Western capital into Poland in the 1970s is an example of a major attempt to resolve the problem. It resulted in a gross misallocation of investment and contributed to Poland's high foreign indebtedness (see, for example, Terrell 1992, 1993).

References

Basu, S., E. Estrin, and J. Švejnar. 1995a. *Employment and Wage Behavior of Enterprises in Transitional Economies.* Photocopy. University of Pittsburgh, 1995b.

———. 1995b. *Employment and Wage Behavior of Industrial Enterprises in Transition.* Photocopy. Washington, D.C.: World Bank.

Boeri, T., and M. Keese. 1992. *Labour Markets and the Transition in Central and Eastern Europe.* Paris: Organization for Economic Cooperation and Development (OECD).

Boeri, T., and S. Scarpetta. 1995. "Emerging Regional Labour Market Dynamics in Central and Eastern Europe." In *The Regional Dimension of Unemployment in Transition Countries.* Paris: OECD.

Bohata, M., P. Hanel, and M. Fischer. "Performance of Manufacturing." In *The Czech Republic and Economic Transition in Eastern Europe,* J. Švejnar, ed. San Diego: Academic Press, pp. 255–284.

Brabant, J. M. van, ed. 1993. *The New Eastern Europe in the Global Economy.* Boulder, Colorado: Westview Press.

Brada, J., and I. Singh. 1994. *Transformation and Labor Productivity in Central and Eastern Europe.* Photocopy. Washington, D.C.: World Bank.

Garner, T.I., and K. Terrell. 1998. "A Gini Decomposition Analysis of Inequality in the Czech and Slovak republics during the Transition." *Economics of Transition,* 6(1):23–46.

Ham, J., J. Švejnar, and K. Terrell. 1995a. "Czech Republic and Slovakia." In *Unemployment, Restructuring and the Labor Market in Eastern Europe and Russia,* S. Commander and F. Coricelli, eds. Washington, D.C.: World Bank, pp. 91–146.

———. 1995b. "Unemployment Duration of Czech and Slovak Men: Evidence from Micro Data." Draft, September.

Kotrba, J. 1995. "Privatization Process in Czech Republic: Players and Winners." In *The Czech Republic and Economic Transition in Eastern Europe,* J. Švejnar, ed. San Diego: Academic Press, pp. 159–198.

Lizal, L., M. Singer, and J. Švejnar. 1995. "Manager Interests, Breakups and Performance of State Enterprises in Transition." In *The Czech Republic and Economic Transition in Eastern Europe,* J. Švejnar, ed. San Diego: Academic Press, pp. 211–232.

———. 1996. *Enterprise Breakups and Restructuring in the Transition.* Photocopy. Ann Arbor, Michigan: William Davidson Institute, December.

Munich, D., J. Švejnar, and K. Terrell. 1995. "Unemployment Dynamics in the Czech and Slovak Republics." In *The Czech Republic and Economic*

Transition in Eastern Europe, J. Švejnar, ed. San Diego: Academic Press, pp. 285–316.

Terrell, K. 1992. "Productivity of Western and Domestic Capital in Polish Industry." *Journal of Comparative Economics* 16(3): 494–514.

———. 1993. "Technological Change and Factor Bias in Polish Industry 1962–1983." *Review of Economics and Statistics* 75(4): 741–746.

Zemplinerova, A., and J. Stibal. 1995. "Evolution and Efficiency of Concentration in Manufacturing." In *The Czech Republic and Economic Transition in Eastern Europe*, J. Švejnar, ed. San Diego: Academic Press, pp. 233–254.

Table 1 Growth in Real GDP in Selected Transition Economies (%)

Country	1990	1991	1992	1993	1994	1995	1996	1997[a]
Czech Republic	–1.6	–11.5	–3.3	0.6	3.2	6.4	3.9	1.0
Hungary	–3.5	–11.9	–3.1	–0.6	2.9	1.5	1.3	4.4
Poland	–11.6	–7.0	2.6	3.8	5.2	7.0	6.1	6.9
Slovakia	–1.6	–14.6	–6.5	–3.7	4.9	6.9	6.6	6.5
Slovenia	–4.7	–8.9	–5.5	2.8	5.3	4.1	3.1	3.8
Bulgaria	–4.3	–11.7	–7.3	–1.5	1.8	2.1	–10.9	–6.9
Romania	–5.6	–12.9	–8.8	1.5	3.9	7.1	3.9	–6.6
Russia	–2.0	5.0	–14.5	–8.7	12.7	4.1	3.5	0.8
Ukraine	–2.6	–11.6	–13.7	–14.2	–23.0	–12.2	–10.0	–3.2
China	3.7	9.5	14.6	13.9	13.0	10.7	9.9	8.8
Vietnam	5.1	6.0	8.6	8.1	8.8	9.5	9.3	8.8

SOURCE: European Bank for Reconstruction and Development, *Transition Report 1998* (London: EBRD, 1998); European Bank for Reconstruction and Development, *Transition Report 1997* (London: EBRD, 1997); and DataStream International (EIU).

[a] EBRD estimates, except China and Vietnam (which are Economist Intelligence Unit estimates).

Table 2 Inflation[a] in Selected Transition Economies (%)

Country	1991	1992	1993	1994	1995	1996	1997[b]	1998[c]
Czech Republic	52.0	12.7	18.2	9.7	7.9	8.6	10.0	9.0
Hungary	32.2	21.6	21.1	21.2	28.3	19.8	18.4	13.5
Poland	60.4	44.3	37.6	29.4	21.6	18.5	13.2	10.0
Slovakia	58.3	9.1	25.1	11.7	7.2	5.4	6.4	9.0
Slovenia	247.1	92.9	22.8	19.5	9.0	9.0	8.8	7.0
Bulgaria	338.9	79.4	63.8	121.9	32.9	310.8	578.5	10.0
Romania	222.8	199.2	295.5	61.7	27.8	56.9	151.4	45.0
Russia	161.0	2,506.1	840.0	204.4	128.6	21.8	10.9	150.0
Ukraine	161.0	2,730.0	10,155.0	401.0	182.0	40.0	10.0	22.0
China	3.6	6.3	14.6	24.2	17.1	8.3	2.8	–0.8[d]
Vietnam	82.7	37.7	8.4	9.3	16.8	5.6	3.1	n.a.[e]

SOURCE: European Bank for Reconstruction and Development, *Transition Report 1998* (London: EBRD, 1998): DataStream International (EIU); and *The Economist* (January 9, 1999).

[a] Measured as the change in year-end retail/consumer price level.

[b] EBRD estimates, except China and Vietnam (EIU estimates).

[c] EBRD projections, except China (*The Economist*).

[d] Year-on-year change in price level, as of December (*The Economist*).

[e] n.a.= not available.

Table 3 Unemployment[a] in Selected Transition Economies (%)

Country	1991	1992	1993	1994	1995	1996	1997[b]	1998[c]
Czech Republic	4.1	2.6	3.5	3.2	2.9	3.5	5.2	7.2
Hungary	7.4	12.3	12.1	10.4	10.4	10.5	10.4	9.3
Poland	11.8	13.6	16.4	16.0	14.9	13.2	10.5	10.0
Slovakia	n.a.[d]	n.a.	12.2	13.7	13.1	11.1	11.6	14.0
Slovenia	8.2	11.5	14.4	14.4	13.9	13.9	14.4	15.0
Bulgaria	11.1	15.3	16.4	12.8	11.1	12.5	13.7	14.6
Romania	3.0	8.2	10.4	10.9	9.5	6.6	8.8	12.0
Russia	0.0	4.8	5.3	7.1	8.3	9.2	10.9	9.3
Ukraine	0.0	0.36	0.4	0.4	0.5	1.1	2.3	4.5
China	2.3	2.3	2.6	2.8	2.9	3.0	5.0	5.0

SOURCE: European Bank for Reconstruction and Development, *Transition Report 1998* (London: EBRD, 1998): and DataStream International (EIU, IFS).

[a] Measured as end-of-year unemployment rate.

[b] EBRD estimates, except China (EIU estimate).

[c] WDI estimates.

[d] n.a. = not available.

Table 4 General Government Balances[a] in Selected Transition Economies (% of GDP)

Country	1990	1991	1992	1993	1994	1995	1996	1997[b]	1998[c]
Czech Republic	n.a.[d]	–1.9	–3.1	0.5	–1.2	–1.8	–1.2	–2.1	–2.4
Hungary	0.4	–2.9	–6.8	–5.5	–8.4	–6.7	–3.1	–4.9	–4.9
Poland	3.1	–6.7	–6.7	–3.1	–3.1	–2.8	–3.3	–3.1	–3.1
Slovakia	n.a.	n.a.	n.a.	–7.0	–1.3	0.2	–1.9	–3.8	–4.0
Slovenia	–0.3	2.6	0.2	0.3	–0.2	0.0	0.3	–1.1	–1.0
Bulgaria	n.a.	n.a.	–5.2	–10.9	–5.8	–5.6	–10.4	–2.1	–2.0
Romania	1.0	3.3	–4.6	–0.4	–1.9	–2.6	–4.0	–3.6	–5.5
Russia	n.a.	n.a.	–4.1	–7.4	–9.0	–5.7	–8.3	–7.4	–8.0
Ukraine	n.a.	n.a.	–25.4	–16.2	–9.1	–7.1	–3.2	–5.6	–3.0
China	n.a.	–1.1	–1.0	–0.9	–1.2	–1.0	–0.7	–0.7	n.a.
Vietnam	–5.8	–1.5	–2.4	–4.8	–1.7	–1.3	–0.6	–1.8	n.a.

SOURCE: European Bank for Reconstruction and Development, *Transition Report 1998* (London: EBRD, 1998); European Bank for Reconstruction and Development, *Transition Report 1997* (London: EBRD, 1997); and DataStream International (EIU).

[a] "General government" includes the state, municipality, and extrabudgetary funds.

[b] EBRD estimates, except China and Vietnam (EIU estimates).

[c] EBRD projections.

[d] n.a. = not available.

Table 5 Foreign Direct Investment[a] (US$, millions)

Country	1990	1991	1992	1993	1994	1995	1996	1997[b]	1998[c]
Czech Republic	n.a.[d]	n.a.	1,000.0	600.0	700.0	2,500.0	1,400.0	1,300.0	1,000.0
Hungary	300.0	1,500.0	1,500.0	2,300.0	1,100.0	4,500.0	2,000.0	2,100.0	1,500.0
Poland	0.0	100.0	300.0	600.0	500.0	1,100.0	2,800.0	3,000.0	4,000.0
Slovakia	n.a.	80.0	100.0	110.0	240.0	190.0	200.0	50.0	220.0
Slovenia	0.0	41.0	113.0	111.0	128.0	176.0	186.0	321.0	200.0
Bulgaria	n.a.	56.0	42.0	40.0	105.0	82.0	100.0	497.0	300.0
Romania	18.0	37.0	73.0	97.0	341.0	417.0	263.0	1,224.0	900.0
Russia	n.a.	n.a.	n.a.	n.a.	500.0	1,700.0	1,700.0	3,800.0	1,500.0
Ukraine	n.a.	n.a.	200.0	200.0	100.0	400.0	500.0	600.0	700.0
China	n.a.	4,370.0	11,160.0	27,520.0	33,790.0	35,850.0	40,180.0	n.a.	n.a.
Vietnam	16.0	229.0	385.0	523.0	742.0	1,400.0	500.0	n.a.	n.a.

SOURCE: European Bank for Reconstruction and Development, *Transition Report 1998* (London: EBRD, 1998); European Bank for Reconstruction and Development, *Transition Report 1997* (London: EBRD, 1997); and World Bank's 1998 World Development Indicators CD-ROM.

[a] Net inflows recorded in the balance of payments.

[b] EBRD estimates.

[c] EBRD projections.

[d] n.a. = not available.

Table 6 Investor Ratings of Countries[a]

Country	1993 15 Nov.	1994 15 Nov.	1995 15 Nov.	1996 12 Nov.	1997 14 Nov.	1998 12 Nov.
Czech Republic	BBB	BBB	A	A	A	A–
Hungary	BB+	BB+	BB+	BBB–	BBB–	BBB–
Poland	n.a.[b]	n.a.	n.a.	BBB–	BBB–	BBB–
Slovakia	n.a.	BB–	BB–	BBB–	BBB–	BBB–
Slovenia	n.a.	n.a.	n.a.	A	A	A–
Romania	n.a.	n.a.	n.a.	BB–	BB–	BB+
Latvia	n.a.	n.a.	n.a.	n.a.	BBB	A–
Lithuania	n.a.	n.a.	n.a.	n.a.	BBB–	BBB–
Russia	n.a.	n.a.	n.a.	BB–	BB–	CCC
China	BBB	BBB	BBB	BBB	BBB+	BBB+

SOURCE: Standard & Poor's *Rating Handbook* and Standard & Poor's *Global Rating Handbook*, various years.

[a] Long-term ratings of sovereign debt in foreign currencies.

[b] n.a. = not available.

6 Reforming the Welfare State in Postsocialist Economies

János Kornai
Harvard University and *Collegium Budapest*

When I was invited to participate in this series on transition, I was not sure whether my proposed topic would really be appropriate. In this paper, I will primarily discuss welfare reform in postsocialist economies. While welfare reform is part of transformation, I do not consider it part of transition. So let me begin by answering the questions of when transition can be considered to be over in general and whether it is over in Hungary specifically. Then I will try to explain the role of welfare reform in the transformation and go on to discuss welfare in detail, with special attention to health care.

Each of us who works in the area has his or her own criteria for determining the end of transition. I have three such criteria, based on the theory I applied in my book, *The Socialist System* (Kornai 1992). When defining socialism, the starting point is not state ownership, central planning, or the communist economy; it is the omnipotent rule of the Communist Party. So the first criterion is that the Communist Party must lose its monopoly power in politics. In that sense, transition in China is definitely not over. One cannot even speak of China as a transition economy because the Communist Party is still in power; rather, China is a reforming communist country. Note that the criterion is not that the country be a democracy, only that the Communist Party not hold a monopoly on political power. The second criterion is that the dominant part of the means of production must be held privately, and the private sector must account for the larger part of gross domestic product (GDP). This private sector does not have to be created exclusively through privatization: it can become dominant through the entry of more and more new firms. Third, the market must be the dominant coordinator of economic activities, alongside various other mechanisms. With these criteria, I aim at a minimum, not at an exhaustive, list.

According to these criteria, the transition from the socialist to the capitalist system in Hungary is basically finished. This conclusion does not mean that there are not any legacies of the former communist system that still need to be transformed; it cannot be stated that everything has been accomplished in all dimensions or that Hungary has a perfect system. There are still many institutions and organizations, as well as attitudes, that must be changed. So transformation is not over, but transition is: the system is now a capitalist one.

Assar Lindbeck, in a recent paper on the Swedish welfare state, refers to Sweden as a country in a mini-transition (Lindbeck 1998). He maintains that the scope as well as the size of the state should be reduced, and most importantly, that the role of the state should be redefined; this is similar to what needs to be done in Hungary. In that sense, one can say that, if Sweden is in transition, Hungary's transition is decidedly not complete, as the reform of the welfare state is still on the agenda. My view, however, is that the reform of the welfare state is part of the ongoing transformation process and that there still are various institutions in need of change in Hungary. Welfare reform is part of the transformation taking place in the postsocialist economies. As the problems in these economies are in some sense similar to those in other countries, from Western Europe through North America to India and China, my suggestions apply to many of the controversies occurring wherever the need for reforming the welfare system is in the forefront of interest.

POINT OF DEPARTURE: PRINCIPLES

Reforming the welfare state is on the political agenda all over the world. For example, there is an ongoing debate over the social security system in the United States. The scope of this paper, however, is limited to the issue of reforming the welfare state in postcommunist countries; that is, the countries that before 1990 were dominated by the Communist Party and operated according to the principles of the communist system, and that are now going through the transformation process. Hungary, my native country, is my main example, but many of my observations and recommendations could be applied to other post-communist countries as well.

Some clarification is needed in terminology. The term *welfare program* means something different in the United States than in many other parts of the world, including Europe. In the United States, *welfare* means social assistance to a certain group of people, particularly people in need. I use the term *welfare state* in a much broader sense; it includes state provision of old-age income ("social security" in U.S. parlance),[1] governmental participation in health provision, support for families, children and mothers, the poor, and also the financing of education. All of these belong under the general term *welfare state activities*, on which this paper focuses in general. In addition, specific attention will be given to reform of the health sector.

A typical point of departure for discussions on welfare reform is the financial soundness of the welfare sector. For example, the first argument when discussing social security in America is that the system is not fiscally sustainable. Other arguments are that the tax burden related to the welfare state is too high and that the welfare sector is not efficient and weakens the incentives for saving. These are all economic issues. There are also political considerations. What would the population accept? What is politically feasible?

Economic and political considerations are extremely important. Nevertheless, reforming the welfare sector has a direct impact on people's lives: how citizens relate to the state, how one relates to fellow citizens, and the nature of citizens' responsibility for their own lives. Here, one has to turn to political philosophy and ethics. Such inquiry is not common for economists, even for those who make policy recommendations.

The usual approach is that economists develop propositions that are consistent with economic principles, and then it is the politicians' duty to implement these ideas. Looking into the philosophical and political ramifications of these propositions is regarded as the job of philosophers and political scientists. In response to that approach, I would distinguish two situations: doing positive economic research and thinking about normative questions in order to formulate policy recommendations. When observing the facts and drawing conclusions and generalizations in order to explain various phenomena, ethical principles can be brushed aside. I would say that 80 percent of my research work has been in positive economics, and in these studies I do not discuss my ethical convictions.

It is quite a different social role, however, if one steps out from the position of an observer and analyst and takes on the responsibility of submitting policy recommendations to the government or to the public. In doing so, the ethical principles behind the suggestions cannot be ignored. There are two tactics economists apply to establish such principles. Many make some tacit or implicit ethical assumptions, leaving them disguised or hidden, so that they are revealed only by careful reading. Others declare openly the ethical principles behind their recommendations.

I am in favor of the latter tactic. There is certainly no consensus about the selection of principles, but being explicit makes one think about them. In the case of some technical issues, one can be technocratic and neutral, but I do not believe that you can make policy recommendations on matters such as welfare state reform without adhering to some basic ethical principles.

I will discuss three of the principles that underly my recommendations.[2] Principle 1 is respect for individual sovereignty. The individual should be his or her own master and must have the right to choose; however, these rights are coupled with an obligation to take responsibility for one's own life. For an American, that seems an almost self-evident principle, but it is much less trivial, for example, in a Scandinavian country, and even less so in a communist country. The communist system was characterized by a lack of respect for individual sovereignty and by strong limitations on choice; at the same time, the individual was relieved of responsibility for his own life. The state said, "You just work and consume what we give you, and we will care for you and tell you what to do." It was the paternalistic state in its extreme, fully patronizing the individual. Great respect of individual sovereignty represents a radical departure from the ingrained beliefs and attitudes that prevailed under the communist system. The paternalistic features of the system should be reduced, as should the state's intervention in the life of the individual.

Principle 2 is the moral obligation of solidarity. One has an ethical duty to assist his or her fellow citizen if that individual is in trouble or in need of help. This idea can be illustrated by several aspects of welfare state activities, such as pensions or social assistance. I will use the health sector as an example. The solidarity principle requires that one cannot be indifferent to what is happening to the health of others. One cannot indifferently watch while another human being is suffering because of an inability to pay for health services.

As an application of solidarity, I formulate a special principle for the health sector, something like a corollary to Principle 2. Equal access to basic health care is a fundamental human right. Two adjectives require some comment. One is "equal." I am not egalitarian in my ethical value system: a strict and consistently egalitarian distribution of income and wealth would be incompatible with Principle 1, as it contradicts the right to individual choice and individual autonomy. However, health deserves special treatment because it is a matter of life and death. People can die if they do not get sufficient health care. Nobel prize-winning economist James Tobin coined the term *specific egalitarianism* regarding basic needs (Tobin 1970). While rejecting egalitarian principles in general, I am ready to accept specific egalitarian principles concerning health.

The second important adjective in my corollary is "basic." I do not suggest equal access to *all* health services; rather, I require only equal access to *basic* health services. I will elaborate upon this concept subsequently, but at this point I only want to emphasize that the corollary implies equal access for everyone to a minimum package.

Principle 1 and Principle 2 are conflicting, and this conflict can be very serious. Therefore, the art of politics is to find an appropriate compromise between these two principles. To do that, certain procedures and institutions are needed, leading to Principle 3, the <u>commitment to democracy and to the transparency of public decision-making processes</u>. Here I will not take positions about whether the total financing that goes to the health sector in, for example, Hungary or Bulgaria or Russia is too much or too little. My concern is not whether health care is overfinanced or underfinanced, which is the main issue in health controversies in Eastern Europe. My question is, who has the right to decide what is too much and what is too little, or more exactly, what institutions and procedures should decide on the magnitude of expenditures on health care.

The answer is not easy, because the players—such as the government, the lawmakers, the doctors, various associations of doctors, centralized insurance institutions, decentralized insurance companies, hospitals, the patient, the taxpayer, trade unions, and employers' associations—have partly common, partly conflicting interests. However, establishing the right procedures and institutions enables the players to decide both the revenues and expenditures of the health sector. My recommendation is to design or to let evolve institutions that will then make these decisions.

INITIAL CONDITIONS

The initial conditions of reform are complex and I will discuss only two. In Eastern Europe and in the republics of the former Soviet Union, there are universal entitlements. These entitlements generally apply to the welfare sector, and especially to health care. A citizen is entitled by the constitution to free medical service. This entitlement is built into his expectations, and his behavior is based on these expectations. Thus, any reduction in the state's responsibility is perceived as a deprivation, a loss of acquired rights. There are many legal problems and constitutional compromises involved in the reform of such a system.

The initial conditions for the reform differ from country to country, so the reformer's approach should vary as well. In the United States, for example, universal health care is not an acquired right. Even China has abandoned the system of universal entitlements. In rural China, where the majority of the Chinese population lives, state commitments ceased with the collapse of the commune system, and health care has been to a very large extent commercialized and turned over to the market. But for Eastern Europe, entitlements are still part of the law, and most medical services are still provided free of charge.

Another condition that must be taken into account is a deep dissatisfaction of the population with health care. People are not terribly grateful for the fact that medical service is free because they take this for granted, but they are very angry if the quality of medical service is poor. They compare it to the standards of countries like Austria, Germany, or France. Today, Eastern Europeans travel widely; they have relatives in other countries, and so they have clear notions of the quality of health service in Western Europe. They find it unfair that living in Hungary, or in Bulgaria or Romania, means that one does not get the same health care that a German or a Belgian would get.

There is a rather clear relationship between GDP and the share of health expenditure in GDP, and it is also established that this share grows as GDP grows. Richer nations spend a larger part of their GDP on health. One can draw a regression line based on data from countries around the world to show this relationship and see that Hungary is above the regression line (World Bank 1993). In an earlier paper (Kornai 1997a), I call Hungary a premature welfare state, because its spending on welfare activities far exceeds what is justified by its level of development. In the 1980s, for example, Hungary was much less advanced than the Scandinavian countries, but the Hungarian ratio of welfare expenditures to GDP reached that of Scandinavia.

Nevertheless, Hungarians were and are dissatisfied. They do not accept the idea that Hungary's GDP is smaller than that of more developed countries and that therefore health expenditures should be smaller, too. They feel, quite understandably, that a suffering Hungarian deserves the same treatment as a suffering Austrian or German. So, while there is free allocation of health services, and total health spending is proportional to the resources, people are not happy. This situation is partly due to the illusion that health care is free: individuals are not aware of the fact that it is they, not the state, who pays for it.

What can be done under these circumstances? In a recent book, I outline my recommendations for reform of the health care system in Hungary.[3] I will present a few ideas from this proposal, which will be organized in two sections. First, I will discuss the demand side, that is, the financing of the health sector; then I will turn to the supply side, the delivery of health care.

THE FINANCING OF HEALTH CARE

First, let us consider the financing of the *minimum basic package*. If we accept the principle that every citizen should have equal access to basic health provision, the guarantor must be the state. There are several possible institutional arrangements; I will consider two, which I will designate A and B.

In arrangement A, the state determines by law a basic package of health insurance that is mandatory (such as the required insurance for automobiles, which can be exceeded by voluntary insurance). Citizens may buy this package in a decentralized insurance market. They are free to choose the insurance company, but they must buy the coverage. If certain people are unable to afford it, the state steps in and pays their mandatory insurance, in accord with the solidarity principle. Those who want to do so can buy additional health insurance, as is consistent with the principle of individual sovereignty. If one is ready to pay more, he or she can buy better health service.

In arrangement B, centralized financing for basic health service is retained, resulting in a kind of national health service (sometimes called a single-payer system) based on taxation. Basic health care is financed by the state budget. This system does not exclude the provision of health service on a voluntary basis, which can be provided in a decentralized fashion.

Arrangement A allows for more freedom of choice and more respect for sovereign decisions, while it ensures, through application of the solidarity principle, equal access to all, including the poor. It also has certain disadvantages, such as higher transaction costs. In addition to these factors, the time sequence of reforms must be considered.

I recommend a two-phase reform process. The first step should be the introduction of arrangement B, because it builds on the initial conditions. That achieved, a gradual move to arrangement A, the more decentralized approach, could follow, provided there is sufficient popular support for such a move. The main reason for suggesting this incremental strategy is that I oppose any suggestion that would create an institutional vacuum. Private insurance policies offered by insurance companies, the institutional framework for decentralized private health insurance, appropriate legal regulation, and well-functioning supervisory authorities still do not exist in the field of health care. One cannot have trust in something one does not know. Consequently, people do not have confidence in private insurance. Listening to a valid explanation is not enough; what really changes people's minds is practical experience.

An illustration is provided by pension reform in Hungary (an area where the Hungarian transformation is greatly ahead of that of other postsocialist countries). The first, preparatory step was the introduction of voluntary pension schemes at the beginning of the 1990s to supplement compulsory contributions paid into the central pension fund. A host of privately managed, decentralized pension funds of all sizes sprang up within a short while. These made good use of investment possibilities offered by the market, and their managers gained expertise in financial operations. Also, the funds operated under strict legal supervision. The first decentralized pension funds started to produce handsome returns for members. This evolution also provided some practical experience for the population and created confidence. Thus, when the new, more radical multipillar pension system was introduced in 1997, which shifted a significant part of compulsory contributions into private, decentralized pension funds and insurance companies, people knew what the privatization of the pension system was about.

A similar attitude is required when decentralizing health insurance: rushing ahead may create serious troubles, as, for example, in the Czech Republic (World Health Organization 1997). There, some insurance companies promised too much in order to lure people into private plans and then refused to pay for certain medical activities; the doctors went on strike because they did not get paid. That is the reason why I do not suggest an early deadline for reaching arrangement A. I recommend starting with arrangement B and progressing gradually. Experience will tell when the time has come to introduce legislation to allow a basic health care package to be bought from licensed health insurance companies that have proved to be reliable. The second phase requires experience, appropriate legislation, regulatory mechanisms, and an elaboration of the ways and means of assisting the needy. Success requires an evolutionary, gradualist approach in this context.

The next issue involves defining what I consider to be "basic." If asked, a physician would say that any reasonable medical intervention is basic. As long as an additional dollar spent on health has positive marginal utility, a doctor is inclined to call it basic. Yet, there is no country in the world, not even the richest, that could increase medical expenditures to the level where the marginal utility of one additional dollar is zero. If tomorrow the United States were to spend three times as much as it does now (13–14 percent of GDP), a doctor could still certainly propose one more activity, operation, screening, or preventative method that would contribute to the improvement of health. It is very difficult for doctors to acknowledge the facts of scarcity and ultimate resource constraints.

Let us confine the discussion at this point to arrangement B, that is, financing the provision of basic health care out of tax revenues. There are two genuinely effective constraints. The first involves how much a country can afford to spend on basic health care at its level of development. The second concerns how much the community is willing to pay for this particular expenditure, that is, for the provision of basic health care for all citizens. This decision is not a medical one in the domain of public finance. It must go through the constitutional channel of political decision making, and thus it should be determined by the legislature.

Lawmakers, of course, need support from their constituencies. They can get support in this case only if ordinary citizens have a better understanding of the relationship between state spending and taxes. Let me repeat that Hungarians think health care is free, and they find it unsatisfactory. They are not aware that they pay for it in many ways, including taxes and various compulsory co-payments. Dissatisfaction makes them ask for greater health expenditures without understanding that this commitment requires more revenues and thus higher taxes. Their discontent is created by deception and is futile. Consequently, I advocate more transparency in financing matters.

There are several practical ways to make financing more transparent. My example is Hungary, but some other Central and Eastern European countries with similar institutional conditions have the same problems.

1. In Europe—not only in Hungary but in many Western European countries—the term social *insurance* is often used. In the Hungarian case, I think this usage is wrong and deceiving. What the employer and employee pay for the services provided by social insurance is far from being an insurance premium; it is first of all a redistributive tax. In the case of a true insurance policy bought and sold on the market, an equal premium is paid by the rich and the poor customer alike for the identical policy sold by the same insurance company. In con-

trast, in the so-called social insurance programs, people with higher incomes contribute more.

2. It is disturbing and confusing that the health tax, or contribution as it is now called, is split into two parts, one paid by the employer and the other by the employee. In fact, both parts are components of the total wage bill, the total compensation for work. The situation would be different if employers could choose from different levels of health contributions, including the zero option. In Hungary, however, the contribution paid by employers is calculated according to uniform and mandatory rates. The system would be much more understandable, without putting any additional tax burden on people, if salaries were summed so as to include the employer's contribution for health insurance and then, out of this gross amount, the contribution were deducted as a tax. That would make it clear to employees how much they pay for the health service. Tax withholding should be the responsibility of employers as part of their managerial and accounting obligation. The present "employer's contribution," with the employer paying the employee's insurance, is deceptive.

3. The introduction of an earmarked health care tax would also improve transparency. Empirical observations show that people are more willing to pay certain taxes if they know exactly what the taxes are being collected for (Haynes and Florestano 1994). As an advocate for specific egalitarianism, I call for a redistributive tax for health care, but one that is designated for this purpose. I am certain that people would be more willing to accept a tax that is spent on others' health than on just anything. It is clear that this only means relabeling initially, but it could help people—patient and doctor alike—to understand that the health tax they pay must cover basic health service for everyone.

4. Currently, the distribution of the tax burden is rather unfair. Taxes collected from employees pay the larger part of the revenues to the social insurance fund. There are millions of free

riders; in fact, one-third of the citizens pay two-thirds of total contributions. It would be desirable to broaden the tax base.

5. Introducing patient co-payments and issuing hospital bills would serve to motivate patients to behave efficiently on the demand side. Currently, patients in Hungary leave the hospital without knowing how much their treatment cost. The doctors and nurses do not know this cost either, nor does anyone else. The bill should also state clearly the size of the patient's direct contribution and the amount paid out of the health tax. People would then know what they get for the tax they pay into the health fund. In general, more tax awareness and spending awareness are needed. The community of taxpayers should know that, if they want more basic health services, they have to pay more in health taxes and in co-payments.

6. Finally, a strict one-to-one correspondence should be established between total expenditures for basic health service and total revenues from health taxes and co-payments. In other words, the general budget should not be used to cover deficits in the health fund. In most Eastern European countries, the health budgets, financed theoretically from the social insurance contributions of citizens and operated by semiautonomous institutions, accumulate huge deficits year after year and are bailed out almost automatically by the state budget. The central budget may provide temporary assistance by extending a loan. In the period of transition, which may last for several years, assistance of some kind is decidedly necessary. However, the ultimate goal should be to avoid accumulating a deficit in the health budget.

HEALTH SERVICE DELIVERY

On the supply side, I am suggesting a gradual process of changing ownership and control mechanisms. Currently, the postsocialist countries have a provision system which, at least on the hospital and outpatient clinic level, shows features of a market socialist regime. State-owned hospitals in Hungary resemble state-owned enterprises under Kádár in Hungary or under Gorbachev in the USSR. They are still highly dependent on the state, and there are hundreds of interventions from the bureaucracy. They also have soft budget constraints. If a hospital runs into debt, it is bailed out almost automatically; if not, extremely strong pressure for a bailout arises. In a Hungarian hospital that exceeded its original budget by millions of forints, the doctors went on a hunger strike to force the minister of finance to cover the deficit; they succeeded. A public hospital or outpatient clinic should have a genuine, hard budget constraint. It must be obliged to cover its expenditures out of its revenues.

I would also welcome a law allowing the privatization of hospitals and clinics in an evolutionary fashion, but I would advise against any quick privatization campaign in the health sector. Also, privatization should not be a free gift (saying to someone, for example, "From now on the hospital is yours").

There can be various combinations of public and private entities operating together. Private companies or medical groups should be allowed to take over the provision of various health services. A public hospital could lease out on a contractual basis certain activities, or private medical groups could lease public hospital infrastructure. The main technique of privatization should be the sale of assets. A hospital or an outpatient clinic as a whole could be sold to a reliable buyer, provided the buyer offers appropriate guarantees to run the organization according to the rules set by law. The emergence of private provision in the health sector should not be carried out by following a detailed design; what needs to be done is to create the legal framework and the supervisory agencies, and thus encourage the evolutionary development of the private sector.

The health care system in the postsocialist countries will probably never have a preponderance of private ownership. Not even the United States, which is regarded as having gone the furthest in encouraging private health care provision, has an overly dominant private sector; a very large number of U.S. hospitals are publicly owned. One cannot expect privatization to go as far on the supply side of the health sector as it does in other areas of the economy. However, there is no need to assign proportions of private and public; the proportions will depend on how things evolve.

CONCLUSIONS

In proposing reforms for the health care sector, I have tried to strike a compromise between contradicting principles, by suggesting an approach that offers more choice and more freedom for the individual and at the same time assures social solidarity. Institutional arrangements should share responsibility between the government and citizens. The decision rights should be split among three parties: the legislature, determining the macrobudget of tax-based basic health provision; doctors involved in the micro-allocation; and households that decide on spending above the mandatory tax.

I hope my suggestions will contribute to the discussion. While this—or any—proposal will not please everybody, there are good chances that such reform can gain serious support.

NOTES

The text of this paper was transcribed directly from the author's oral lecture; it therefore carries more of the characteristics of oral presentation.

1. In Europe, the term "social security" is what social policy aims to achieve; in the United States, it means old-age income provided by the state.
2. This discussion is based on a paper in which I elaborate on nine principles (Kornai 1997b).
3. This book has so far been published only in Hungarian.

References

Haynes, Don, and Patricia S. Florestano. 1994. "Public Acceptability of Taxing Alternatives: Evidence from Maryland." *Public Administration Quarterly* 17(4): 447–467.

Kornai, János. 1992. *The Socialist System: The Political Economy of Communism.* Princeton: Princeton University Press; and Oxford: Oxford University Press.

———. 1997a. "The Citizen and the State: Reform of the Welfare System." In *Struggle and Hope: Essays on Stabilization and Reform in a Post-Socialist Economy.* Chaltenham, U.K.: Edward Elgar Publishing.

———. 1997b. "Reform of the Welfare Sector in the Post-Communist Countries: A Normative Approach." In *Transforming Post-Communist Political Economies*, Joan Nelson, Charles Tilly, and Lee Walker, eds. Washington, D.C.: National Academies Press.

Lindbeck, Assar. 1998. *Swedish Lessons for Post-Socialist Countries.* Discussion Paper Series, Collegium Budapest.

Tobin, James. 1970. "On Limiting the Domain of Inequality." *Journal of Law and Economics* 13: 263–277.

World Bank. 1993. *World Development Report 1993: Investing in Health.* New York: Oxford University Press.

World Health Organization (WHO). 1997. *European Health Care Reform: Analysis of Current Strategies.* Robert B. Saltman and Joseph Figueras, eds. WHO Regional Publications, European Series, No. 72.

The Authors

Marie Lavigne

Emeritus Professor of Economics, University of Pau, France, and
Research Fellow, Institute of Applied Mathematics and Economics

Professor Lavigne earned her Ph.D. in economics at the University of Strasbourg, where she also earned an M.A. in Russian Language and Literature. She has taught at the University of Paris and at the University of Strasbourg. She served as Director of the European Studies Center in Czechoslovakia in 1991. She has conducted research both before and after the onset of transition in many countries, including the USSR, Russia, Albania, Bulgaria, Czechoslovakia, the Czech Republic, the GDR, Hungary, Poland, Romania, and Yugoslavia. Professor Lavigne's fields of research are the political economy of socialism, international economic relations of the (former) Soviet Union and Eastern Europe, integration of Eastern Europe in the world economy, and transition to the market in Russia and Eastern Europe. Recently she has expanded her research agenda to include the transition to market and patterns of growth in Vietnam, Laos, and Cambodia. Her most recent book is *The Economics of Transition, from Socialist Economy to Market Economy,* which was published in both English and Spanish.

Alan H. Gelb

Chief Economist, Africa Region, World Bank

Dr. Gelb was a Rhodes Scholar and received his Ph.D. in economics from Oxford University. He is currently Chief Economist for the Africa Region at the World Bank, where he also serves as the regional technical manager for economic management and social policy in the Africa Region at the International Bank for Reconstruction and Development. Dr. Gelb has visited, researched, and advised innumerable developing countries in Africa, Asia, Europe, and Central and South America, including most of the countries considered to be transition economies. He was part of the Joint Study of the USSR, which took place in 1990–91, and was responsible for overseeing the components on agriculture, manufacturing industry, and housing. Dr. Gelb's areas of research have included commodity price stabilization and control, employee ownership and incentive systems in cooperative structures, macroeconomic theory and modeling, rural industrialization in China, financial systems and policies, and systemic reform. He has written and co-edited several books, including the recent *Restructuring and Privatization in Central Eastern Europe: Case Studies of Firms in Transition* and *Oil Windfalls: Blessing or Curse*?

Anders Åslund

Senior Associate, Carnegie Endowment for International Peace

Dr. Åslund graduated from both the Stockholm School of Economics and the University of Stockholm and received his Ph.D. in economic history from Oxford University. From 1989 to 1994, he was Professor and Director of the Stockholm Institute of East European Economies at the Stockholm School of Economics. Dr. Åslund served as an economic advisor to the Russian government from November 1991 until January 1994, and he has been an economic advisor to the Ukrainian government since August 1994. Since the beginning of transition, he has been a primary participant in the policy debates surrounding reform in these countries. He has been a research scholar at the Kennan Institute for Advanced Russian Studies and a guest scholar at The Brookings Institution. He is also a member of two Russian academies and a number of boards of directors and advisory boards. Since he finished his Ph.D. in 1982, Dr. Åslund's several books include *How Russia Became a Market Economy; Gorbachev's Struggle for Economic Reform; Post-Communist Economic Revolutions: How Big a Bang?* and *Private Enterprise in Eastern Europe: The Non-Agricultural Private Sector in Poland and the GDR, 1945–83.*

Nicholas R. Lardy

Senior Fellow, The Brookings Institution

Dr. Lardy received his Ph.D. in economics from the University of Michigan. Prior to his current position at Brookings, Dr. Lardy was Professor and Director of the Henry M. Jackson School of International Studies at the University of Washington. Dr. Lardy serves on the board of directors and executive committee of the National Committee on United States-China Relations; is a member of the Council on Foreign Relations; and is a member of the editorial boards of three journals. His current project at Brookings, *Financial Reform in China's Economic Transition*, will evaluate the reform of China's banking system and measure the economic consequences of deferring economic reform in the state-owned sector. He has written many books, including *China in the World Economy; Foreign Trade and Economic Reform in China, 1978–90; Agriculture in China's Modern Economic Development: A*

Non-Maoist Alternative; Agricultural Prices in China; and *Economic Growth and Distribution in China.*

Jan Švejnar

Executive Director, William Davidson Institute, and
Everett E. Berg Professor of Business and Economics and International Business, University of Michigan Business School

Professor Švejnar received his Ph.D. in economics from Princeton University. He has directed the William Davidson Institute since July 1996. He also holds an appointment as Professor in the Economics Department at the University of Michigan. Concurrently with his present positions in Michigan, he is the Director of the Economics Institute of the Academy of Sciences of the Czech Republic and the chairman of the executive and supervisory committee of the Center for Economic Research and Graduate Education of Charles University in Prague. Professor Švejnar was one of the chief architects of the Czech Republic's economic reforms, and he continues to serve as an advisor to Czech President Václav Havel. His research in economic development has included the effect of government policy on firms' economic performance and the behavior of multinationals and joint ventures. He has written and edited several books and monographs, including *Economic Transformation in Central and Eastern Europe: The Tasks Still Ahead* and *The Czech Republic and Economic Transition in Eastern Europe.*

János Kornai

Allie S. Freed Professor of Economics, Harvard University, and
Permanent Fellow, Collegium Budapest, Institute for Advanced Study

Professor Kornai earned both a Doctor of Economics degree from Karl Marx University of Economics in Budapest and a Doctor of Science degree from the Hungarian Academy of Sciences. In addition to positions at Harvard and the Collegium Budapest, he is a research professor in the Institute of Economics at the Hungarian Academy of Sciences, where he has been doing research for 30 years. Professor Kornai has served on the Scientific Advisory Council of the European Bank for Reconstruction and Development, was vice chairman of the United Nations Committee for Development Planning, and has been president of the Hungarian Social Science Association, the European Economic Association, and the Econometric Society. He is a member of the board of the Hungarian National Bank. He has received the Hungarian State

Prize, the Erasmus Medal, and the Szchényi Prize. His work has been extremely influential, both in the field of Soviet-type economics and in the new study of transition economics. His famous book *The Road to a Free Economy*: *Shifting from a Socialist System: The Example of Hungary* was published in 15 languages. Some of his other books, all published in two or more languages, are *Highways and Byways: Studies on Socialist Reform and Post-socialist Transition*; *Economics of Shortages*; and *Growth, Shortage and Efficiency.*

Annette N. Brown

Assistant Professor, Western Michigan University

Professor Brown attended graduate school at the University of Michigan on a National Science Foundation Fellowship; she received an M.A. in Russian and East European Studies in 1992 and a Ph.D. in economics in 1996. During her graduate studies, she spent two years consulting for the World Bank, including serving on the core team who wrote the *World Development Report 1996: From Plan to Market.* She is currently an associate at the Stockholm Institute of Transition Economics, a research affiliate of the Centre of Economic Policy Research, and a research fellow of the William Davidson Institute. She serves on the editorial board for *Comparative Economic Studies*. Professor Brown's research interests span industrial organization and labor economics topics in transition economies. Most of her current research involves a large project titled *Competition, Reallocation, and Industrial Evolution: Advances in the Economics of Industrial Organization Using Economy-wide Panel Data on Firms in Russia*, being done with colleagues at the Stockholm Institute of Transition Economics.

Author Index

Åslund, Anders, 54, 57, 66n2, 67n7
 career, 1, 2–3, 116
Aven, Petr O., 67

Balcerowicz, Leszek, 63
Basu, S., 82
Blasi, Joseph R., 55
Boeri, T., 87, 91
Bohata, M., 91
Boone, Peter, 54, 57, 67n7
Boss, Helen, 28
Boycko, Maxim, 64
Brabant, J.M., 81
Brada, J., 91
Brown, Annette N., 61, 118
Bruno, Michael, 21

de Melo, Marta, 23
Dmitriev, M.S., 56
Dobrinsky, Rumen, 28

Estrin, E., 82

Fischer, M., 91
Fisher, Stanley, 23
Florestano, Patricia S., 109

Garner, T.I., 82
Geddes, Barbara, 67n6
Gelb, Alan H., 23
 career, 2, 3, 115–116
Gligorov, Vladimir, 28
Goldman, Marshall I., 52
Granville, Brigitte, 67n4

Ham, J., 91
Hanel, P., 91
Havlik, Peter, 28
Haynes, Don, 109
Hellman, Joel, 66
Hunya, Gábor, 28

Ickes, Barry, 61

Johnson, Simon, 54, 57, 67n7

Kaufmann, Daniel, 52, 64
Keese, M., 87
Kornai, János, 16, 18, 63, 99, 105, 112n2
 career, 1, 2, 117–118
Kotrba, J., 91
Kroumova, Maya, 55
Kruse, Douglas, 55
Kuzes, Irina Y., 52

Lardy, Nicholas R., 2, 3, 116–117
Laski, Kazimierz, 28
Lavigne, Marie, 28
 career, 1, 2, 115
Layard, Richard, 67n4
Lindbeck, Assar, 100
Lipton, David, 63
Lizal, L., 91
Lukas, Zdenek, 28

Maravall, Jose Maria, 67n7
Marer, Paul, 28
Matovnikov, M. Yu, 56
Mikhailov, L.V., 56
Munich, D., 88

Nelson, Lynn D., 52

Olson, Mancur, 57

Podkaminer, Leon, 33, 35
Pöschl, Josef, 28

Richter, Andrea, 67n4
Richter, Sándor, 28
Rodrik, Dani, 28
Ryterman, Randi, 61

Sachs, Jeffrey D., 27n2, 63

Sahay, Ratna, 23
Scarpetta, S., 91
Shleifer, Andrei, 64, 66
Siegelbaum, Paul, 52, 64
Singer, M., 91
Singh, I., 91
Stibal, J., 92
Švejnar, Jan, 82, 88, 91
  career, 1, 2, 117
Sycheve, L.I., 56

Terrell, K., 82, 88, 90n4, 91
Timofeev, E.V., 56
Tobin, James, 103

Urban, Waltraut, 28

Vegh, Carlos A., 23
Vidovic, Hermine, 28
Vishny, Robert, 64, 66

Warner, A., 56
Williamson, John, 27n3

Zemplinerova, A., 92

Subject Index

Acquis communautaire, 27, 28n5
Albania, 15, 23
  economic and social data, 30, 32, 34, 36
Arbitrage, 53, 59, 62
Armenia, 40
Asian countries in transition
  geopolitical grouping of, 15
  reforms needed in, 47–49
  rent-seeking in, 58
  See also China; Vietnam
Asian model of transition, 79
Attitudes and transition, 6, 18, 22, 25, 60–61, 106–107
Autarky, 17
Azerbaijan, 60

Bad debts. *See* Nonperforming loans
Balance of trade and payments deficits, 84
Balkan states, 59
Baltic states
  geopolitical grouping of, 15
  economic and social data, 30, 32, 34, 36
  differences from other transition countries, 6
  media in, 58
  rent-seeking in, 56, 59, 61–62
  subsidized credit in, 54
  See also Estonia; Latvia; Lithuania
Banking system reforms, 20, 21, 36, 37, 47, 72–75
Banking systems
  Central European countries, 85, 86–87, 89
  China, 45–46, 48, 70–75
  CIS states, 62
  communist vs. market economy, 17
  conflicts of interest in, 89
  problems of, 45
  Russia, 56, 60–61
Bank managers, 18, 56, 86
Bankruptcy, 21, 25, 37, 89
Basic health care
  defining, 103, 107–108
  financing of, 105
Belarus
  economic and social data, 30, 33, 34, 36
  foreign aid to, 65
  rent-seeking in, 62, 64
  net revenues from credit issue, 54
Big bang model of economic reform, 19, 20
Black market, 24
Budget cuts, 65
Budget deficits
  acceptable levels of, 22
  in Central European countries, 78, 96
  in China, 71, 79, 96
  curbing, 20
  in former Soviet Union, 78–79
  for health care, 110
  rent-seeking and, 58, 60, 64
  in selected transition countries, 96
  in Vietnam, 79, 96
Building blocks for transition, 19–22, 85–90
Bulgaria
  economic and social data, 30, 32, 34, 36, 93–97
  economic problems in, 79
  geopolitical grouping of, 15
  health care system, 104–105
  reforms in, 19, 21, 23, 64
Bureaucracy, 24, 111

Cambodia, 15
Capital, availability of, 85
Capital account transaction convertibility, 74
Capital flight, 46, 66n2, 86

Capital flows
  Central European countries vs. China, 81
  EU stipulations about, 27
  need for unprotected, 77
  short-term inflows, 22, 34–35
  See also Foreign direct investment
Capital markets
  in China, 70
  in former Soviet Union, 59
  importance of, 20
  in transition countries, 36, 37
Caucasus, 59
CEE. *See* Central and Eastern Europe
Central and Eastern Europe
  definition of, 6, 15
  economic and social data, 30–38
  EU membership conditions for, 26–27
  legacy of Soviet strategies, 17
  macroeconomic crisis, 43
  money overhang in, 43
  output rates, 22
  pace of liberalization, 43
  past policy decisions, 45, 46
  rate of GDP growth, 79
  reforms in, 40–41, 42–43, 47–49
  rent-seeking in, 56
  response to liberalization, 44
  unemployment rates, 22
  See also Central European countries; Former Soviet Union; individual nations
Central Asia, 59
Central European countries
  definition of, 6, 15, 90n1
  media in, 58
  pension systems, 88
  principal aspects of transition in, 80–84
  See also Czech Republic; Hungary; Poland; Slovakia
Central European model of transition, 77–98
Central planning, 17, 77, 80–81
Chernomyrdin, Viktor, 61
China
  banking system reform, 72–75
  compared with other transition countries, 6, 81
  economic indicators, 93–98
  FDI in, 70, 79, 95
  geopolitical grouping of, 15
  health care system, 104
  integration into world economy, 70
  investment-grade rating, 70
  labor force, 48
  levels of investment, 83
  model of transition, 79
  money overhang in, 43
  pace of liberalization, 43, 69
  pattern of growth, 44–45
  pension systems, 88
  policy decisions, 45–46
  prospects for future recession, 75–76
  recession in, 75
  reforms in, 40–43, 48
  social safety net, 82
  state-owned enterprises (SOEs), 82
  transition country status, 99
  unemployment rates, 79, 90n3, 95
  unsustainable economic strategy, 70–72
CIS. *See* Commonwealth of Independent States
Civil society
  developing, 6
  rent-seeking and, 58
CMEA. *See* Council for Mutual Economic Assistance
Collective ownership. *See* State ownership
Comecon. *See* Council for Mutual Economic Assistance
Commodity traders, rent-seeking and, 56
Commonwealth of Independent States (CIS)
  rate of GDP growth, 79–80

reforms in, 15, 20
relative economic stability, 62
rent-seeking in, 56, 59, 61–62
Communism
as cause of rent-seeking, 57
and individual sovereignty, 102
legacies of, 16, 104–105
Communist Party, 16–17, 57–58, 99
Corporate governance, 24, 38, 46, 89
Corruption, 24, 26, 46, 62, 87
See also Crime
Council for Mutual Economic Assistance (CMEA, Comecon), 17, 81
Credit policies, 37, 38
Crime, 24, 55
See also Corruption
Croatia, 77
Currency
devaluation, 21, 66, 81, 84
domestic, 21, 37, 74
foreign, 20
Currency boards, 20–21
Current account balances, 22, 34–35
Current account convertibility, 21, 37
Czech Republic
balanced budget, 78
banking system, 89
bankruptcy rates, 89
budget deficit, 22
economic and social data, 30, 32, 34, 36, 93–98
economic policies, 48
economic problems in, 79
economic recovery by, 46
exchange rate policies, 84
foreign debt, 83
geopolitical grouping of, 15
levels of investment, 83
poor economic performance (1996–1998), 84
privatization in, 89
progress of transition in, 78, 79
reforms in, 23, 42, 63, 107
relative financial stability, 60
rent-seeking in, 58, 59
sovereign debt ratings, 78
state-owned enterprises (SOEs), 82
unemployment rate, 22, 25, 78, 82–83, 87, 95
voucher system, 21, 40, 49, 83
See also Klaus, Vaclav

Debt
of state-owned enterprises, 70, 111
writing off bad, 73
See also Gross debt; Savings account build-ups; Sovereign debt
Decision-making, health care, 103–104, 108, 110–111, 112
Defaults
on foreign aid, 60, 66
on household liabilities, 72
on loans. *See* Nonperforming loans
Defense expenditures. *See* Military vs. consumer goods production
Deficits
balance of trade and payments deficits, 84
public sector nonfinancial deficit, 71
See also Budget deficit
Democracy
and economic reforms, 57–58
and rent-seeking, 64
and transition, 6, 26, 99, 103–104
vulnerability to false promises, 25
Demographic/social data, transition countries, 30–31
De-monopolization, 17, 37
Deng Xiapoing era, 71
Devaluation of currencies, 21, 66, 81, 84
Dictatorships and rent-seeking, 58
Domestic currency, 21, 37, 74
Domestic securities, 21, 38, 87
Domestic trade, 20, 60

Eastern European countries
geopolitical grouping of, 15
organized crime in, 24
and universal entitlements, 104

Eastern European countries (cont.)
  See also Bulgaria; Romania; Russia; Slovenia
EBRD. *See* European Bank for Reconstruction and Development
Economic contraction, 44
Economic distortions, 59
Economic indicators
  biased reporting of, 90n2
  monetary-financial, 22, 30–35, 93–98
  See also GDP
Economic misconceptions, 60–61
Economic reform, 14
  banking system, 20, 21, 36, 37, 47, 72–75
  big bang model for, 19, 20
  cumulative exposure to, 41
  debate over pace of, 19
  driving forces behind, 42–43
  educational system, 25, 47, 87
  ethical principles for, 100–104
  factors influencing pace of, 43, 49, 64
  fast-paced, 44
  future agenda of, 47–49
  gradual, 57–58, 61, 69–76, 106–107
  health care system, 81–82, 101, 103, 104–113
  importance of moving toward, 19–20
  influence of democracy on, 57–58
  initial conditions of, 104–105
  liberalization/stabilization stage, 6, 19–21
  need for simultaneous, 41–42, 71–72
  outcomes of, 44–46
  structural stage, 6, 21–22, 36–38
  success of partial, 63, 66
  See also Structural transformation; Transition
Education
  educational system reforms, 25, 47, 87
  in communist systems, 16, 19
  indicators, 18, 30–31
Egalitarian distribution of income, 16, 69
Egalitarianism, specific, 103, 109
Employment adjustment, 82–83
Energy sector
  incomes from, 56
  prices, 20, 53
  rent-seeking and, 60
  subsidies, 46
Enterprise restructuring, 36–37, 80, 81, 86–87
  as transition criterion, 99
Entitlements, 104
Entrepreneurial skills, barriers to, 18
Environmental policies, 20
Equilibrium, long-run market, 10
Estonia
  economic and social data, 30, 32, 34, 36
  and EU membership, 38
  geopolitical grouping of, 15
  net revenues from credit issue, 54
  reforms in, 20–21, 42, 63
  rent-seeking in, 58
EU. *See* European Union
Eurocentric approach, 39
European Bank for Reconstruction and Development (EBRD), 83
European Community, trade with, 81
European Union (EU)
  countries applying for membership in, 15, 23–24, 37, 38
  importance for transition, 14
  membership conditions, 7, 26–27, 39, 47, 89–90
  as scapegoat, 25
Exchange rates
  in Central European countries, 83–84, 86
  liberalization of, 37
  multiple, 37, 53
  in Soviet Union (1991), 60
  stabilization of, 20, 22
  unification of, 62, 63

Exports
  Central European countries, 84, 89
  data on, 34–35
  of manufactured goods, 81
  ratio to GDP, 17
  rents from, 53, 55, 56
Extortion, 60–61, 62

Farms. *See* Landholding and transition
FDI. *See* Foreign direct investment
Fedorov, Boris, 63
Financial balances and liberalization, 43
Financial crisis and rent-seeking, 60, 65
Financial data, 34–35
Financial markets, 21, 41
Financial system reforms, 47, 70–76
Financing of health care, 105–110
Fiscal reform
  in Central European countries, 88
  in China, 73–76
Foreign aid
  to Belarus, 65
  Soviet Union default (1991), 60, 66
Foreign direct investment (FDI), 26
  in Central European countries, 85–86, 97
  in China, 70, 79, 97
  data on, 34–35
  in East Asian countries, 85
  EU stipulations about, 27
  in former Soviet Union, 78–79
  in transition countries, 34–35, 97
Foreign exchange liberalization, 20, 36–37
Foreign financial institutions, 74, 76n1, 87
Foreign trade. *See* International trade
Former Soviet Union
  decline in output of, 22
  definition of, 6, 15
  exclusion from EU, 14
  falling productivity in 1960s, 42
  lagging transition of, 23
  legacies of, 16–19, 104–105
  macroeconomic crisis, 43
  model of transition, 78–79
  money overhang in, 43
  organized crime in, 24
  reforms in, 40–41, 42–44
  rent-seeking in, 51–68
  See also Commonwealth of Independent States; Russia
Freedom
  for the individual, 102
  of the press, 26

Gaidar, Yegor, 63
Gazprom, 53, 65
GDP. *See* Gross domestic product.
Geography, economic recovery role of, 46
Gierek, Edward, 90n4
Gini coefficient, 31, 49
Gini index. *See* Gini coefficient
Government. *See* State
Government bonds
  trading in, 38
  using to recapitalize banks, 73–74
Gradualist model of economic reform, 19, 106–107
Gross debt, 34–35
Gross domestic product
  growth of, 84–90, 93
  health expenditures and, 105
  indexes of, 32–33
  former Soviet Union, 51
  output losses, 44
  ratio of exports to, 17
  state spending and, 47, 48
Gross rents, 54, 62
Growth
  barriers to, 46
  and liberalization, 23
  sustaining high rates of, 84–90
  See also Sustainable growth

Havel, Vaclav, 2

Health care
  equal access to, 103
  financing of, 105–110
  system reform, 103–105
Health insurance, 107
Heterodox approach to stabilization, 21
History, economic recovery role of, 46
Household savings account build-ups, 43, 45, 71, 72, 74, 75
Housing, 17, 19, 20
Human capital
  in China, 48
  development of, 87
  planned economy's legacy, 18
Human Development Index, 4, 18, 22, 30–31
Hungary
  bank recapitalization, 73
  bankruptcy rates, 89
  central planning, 77
  economic and social data, 30, 32, 34, 36, 93–98
  economic stagnation, 78
  exchange rate policies, 84
  foreign direct investment, 85–86
  foreign debt, 83
  geopolitical grouping of, 15
  health care system reform, 104–110
  human welfare expenditures in, 105
  levels of investment in, 83
  pension reform in, 107
  privatization in, 21
  public expenditures, 88
  relative financial stability, 60
  rent-seeking in, 58, 59
  sovereign debt ratings in, 78
  state-owned enterprises (SOEs), 82
  strength of civil society, 58
  transition declared finished, 100
  unemployment rate, 82, 95
Hyperinflation, 54, 61, 72, 78

IMF. *See* International Monetary Fund

Imports
  data on, 34–35
  liberalization of, 81
  subsidies for, 53, 56
Income
  egalitarian distribution of, 16, 69
  inequalities, 24, 46, 49, 52, 55–56, 60, 82
  institutional development and, 39
  necessary short-term reduction, 76
Individual sovereignty, respect for, 102, 112
Indochinese countries in transition, 15
Industry. *See* Production structure
Inflation
  as barrier to transition, 14
  in Central European countries, 22, 78, 94
  in China, 44–45, 69, 79, 94
  from credit subsidies, 53–54
  curbing, 20, 45
  in former Soviet Union, 51, 60
  liberalization and, 23, 43
  data on, 22, 32–34, 94
  rent-seeking and, 58, 63
  sharp economic contraction and, 44
  in Vietnam, 44–45, 79, 94
  See also Hyperinflation
Initial conditions for transition, 2, 16–19, 104–105
Interest rates
  banking reform and, 38
  effect of high, 86
  in former Soviet Union, 59
  data on, 22, 32–34
  restoration of, 21
Interest subsidies, 62
International Monetary Fund. (IMF)
  effect on rent-seeking, 65
  importance to transition, 14
  as scapegoat, 25
  transition package agreements, 19, 22
  Washington consensus, 27n3

International trade
  Central European countries, 80, 83–84
  Central and Eastern European countries, 17
  China's share of, 70
  data on, 22, 34–35
  liberalization of, 20
  rents from, 63–64
  See also Exports; Imports
Investment
  barriers to, 46, 85–87
  Central European countries' levels of, 80, 83, 85–86
  index, 22, 32–34
  promoting, 47
  vehicles for, 38

Joint-stock corporations, Russian, 40

Kazakhstan
  economic and social data, 30, 33, 34, 36
  net revenues from credit issue, 54
  radical reform politics, 64
  rent-seeking in, 60
Klaus, Vaclav, 14
Kleptocracy, 59
Kyrgyz Republic
  economic and social data, 31, 33, 35, 37
  income inequalities in, 55
  net revenues from credit issue, 54
  obstacle to economic recovery, 46

Labor. *See* Human capital; Unemployment; Workers
Labor mobility, 48, 77
Landholding and transition, 10, 40, 43
Laos, 15
Large-scale privatization, 21, 36–37
Latvia
  economic and social data, 30, 32, 34, 36
  geopolitical grouping of, 15
  net revenues from credit issue, 54
  rent-seeking in, 58
Laws and legal systems, 24, 26, 47, 80, 89, 111
Legacies of planned economies, 6, 14–15, 16–19, 25, 104–105
  people's attitudes as, 18, 61, 100
Legal system. *See* Laws and legal system
Liberalization
  effects in Russia, 46, 61
  financial balances and, 43
  as first stage of transition, 6, 20, 40–43
  pace of, 43
  transition countries' responses to, 44
  vs. growth and inflation, 23
  See also Foreign exchange liberalization; Price liberalization; Trade liberalization
Lithuania, 20, 63
  economic and social data, 30, 32, 34, 36
  geopolitical grouping of, 15
  net revenues from credit issue, 54
  rent-seeking in, 58
Loan shortages, 86–87
Loans outstanding, 70–71, 73

Maastricht convergence criteria, 27
Macroeconomic crisis, 43
Macroeconomic data on transition countries, 32–33
Macroeconomic stabilization. *See* Stabilization
Managers
  in Central European countries, 89
  income inequality in Russia and, 55
  legacy attitudes of, 18, 25
  of state-owned enterprises, 17, 89
Manufacturing sector. *See* Production structure
Market economy
  abolition of central planning and, 17
  as criterion for end of transition, 77, 99–100

Market economy (cont.)
different models of, 40
disequilibrium of some features, 10
employment adjustment and, 83
new, 23–27
obstacles to building, 24–26
pace of productive structure changes, 10
publics' need to understand, 6, 60–61
See also Transition
Market reforms, 41
Market socialist regime, 110
Mass privatization, 21, 82, 89
Media, 26, 58
Military vs. consumer goods production, 10, 18, 44, 60
Ministries, communist vs. market economy, 17
Minorities, protection of, 26
Mises, Ludwig von, 64
Mixed economies, 25–26
Moldova, 64
economic and social data, 30, 33, 34, 36
net revenues from credit issue, 54
Monetary policy, 21
Money as source of rents, 53–54
Money overhang, 43, 45, 70–71
Mongolia, 15
Monopolies
creation of private, 17
Russian trade, 61
Moscow stock market, 67n5

National health service, 106
Natural resources and rent-seeking, 60
Newly Independent States (NIS). *See* Former Soviet Union
Nomenklatura, 16–17, 57–58, 99
Nonperforming loans, 48, 70–71, 73

OECD wage replacement rates, 88
Oil/gas and rent-seeking, 60
Organized crime, 24
Orthodox approach to stabilization, 21
Output
falls from rent-seeking, 64–65
measures in transition countries, 22, 32–34

Packages, transition, 19–22
Paternalism, 18, 25, 102
Pension systems, 22, 24, 81–82, 88, 101, 107
People's Bank of China, 74
Performance indicators. *See* Economic indicators
Physical infrastructure, legacy of, 18
Planned economy
deficiencies of, 42
liberalization of, 40–43
Planning mentality, 17
Poland
bankruptcy rates, 89
central planning, 77
economic and social data, 30, 32, 34, 36, 93–98
economic growth pattern, 51
effects of privatization, 55
exchange rate policies, 84
foreign debt, 83, 90n4
geopolitical grouping of, 15
human development, 22
levels of investment, 83
privatization in, 89
public expenditures, 88
reforms in, 42, 63
rent-seeking in, 58, 59
shortages in, 20
social safety nets, 40
state-owned enterprises (SOEs), 82
strength of civil society, 58, 89
Political change, impact of, 42–43
Political philosophy and economics, 101–104
Poverty, 24, 61, 69, 82
Price distortions, 59, 64

Price liberalization
  barriers to, 59
  in Central European countries, 81
  in China, 69
  as criterion for end of transition, 19, 20
  to eliminate arbitrage, 62
  in former Soviet Union, 53–55, 60
  necessity of, 41
  in selected transition countries, 36, 37
Private insurance, 22, 106
Privatization
  barriers to, 17
  in Central European countries, 44, 80, 81, 82
  in China, 69, 75
  data on, 36–37
  as end to rent-seeking, 52, 64
  in former Soviet Union, 44, 48
  of health system, 107
  of hospitals and clinics, 111
  income inequalities and, 55–56
  of land, 10
  stages of, 20, 21
  as transition criterion, 99
  vs. structural transformation, 22–23
  See also Mass privatization
Production imbalances, 10
Production structure
  legacy of distorted, 17
  strengthening China's, 75
Productivity, 19
Professions, creating new, 47
Profit-seeking, 52, 64
Property rights to large assets, 49
Protectionism. *See* Liberalization
Public expenditures, 21
Public policiy
  credit, 37, 38
  economic performance and, 45–46
  effect of income inequality on, 49
  ethical principles and, 101–104
  exchange rate, 83–84, 86
  industrial, 20, 75
  inflationary, 61
  interdependence of, 42
  labor market, 87–88
  monetary, 21
  structural transformation, 20
  transition country, 41
  See also Social safety net
Public sector nonfinancial deficit, 71

Recapitalization of China's banks, 72–74, 75–76
Redistributive taxes, 108–109
Reforms. *See* Economic reforms
Rent-seeking
  causes of, 56–62
  controlling, 62–65
  impact on transition countries, 51–52
  postcommunist, 52–56
Retirement benefits. *See* Pension systems
Romania
  economic and social data, 30, 32, 34, 36, 93–98
  economic problems in, 79
  geopolitical grouping of, 15
  health care system, 104–105
  privatization in, 40
  reforms in, 23, 64
Russia
  central planning, 77
  default on household liabilities, 72
  economic and social data, 30, 33, 34, 36, 93–98
  economic policies, 48
  economic progress (1996–1997), 79
  export rents, 53
  fall of gross rents, 62
  financial crisis, 66
  foreign aid to Belarus, 65
  GDP (1992), 54
  geopolitical grouping of, 15
  implicit social contract legacy, 18
  income inequalities in, 55–56

Russia (cont.)
- joint-stock company farms, 10, 40
- levels of investment, 83
- media in, 58
- model of transition, 78–79
- money supply, 53–54
- net revenues from credit issue, 54
- obstacles to economic recovery, 46
- pension systems, 88
- price liberalization in, 63
- privatization in, 40, 48, 81
- reforms in, 20
- rent-seeking in, 52, 60, 61–62, 66
- state-owned enterprises (SOEs), 82
- subsidized credits, 54–55
- trade monopolies, 61
- unemployment rates, 83, 95
- voucher system, 55

Savings account build-ups, 43, 45, 71, 72, 74, 75
Securities, issuance of, 21, 38, 67n5
Security. *See* Social safety net
Shock therapy model of economic reform, 19, 20
Single-payer system, 106
Skilled labor, legacy of, 18
Slovakia
- balanced budget, 78
- banking system, 89
- bankruptcy rates, 89
- budget deficit, 22
- economic and social data, 30, 32, 34, 36, 93–98
- and EU membership, 38
- exchange rate policies, 84
- geopolitical grouping of, 15
- inflation in, 78, 94
- levels of investment, 83
- privatization in, 89
- rent-seeking in, 59
- sovereign debt ratings, 78
- state-owned enterprises (SOEs), 82
- unemployment rates, 83, 95

Slovenia
- balanced budget, 78
- budget deficit, 22
- central planning, 77
- economic and social data, 30, 32, 34, 36, 93–98
- and EU membership, 38
- foreign debt, 83
- geopolitical grouping of, 15
- inflation in, 78, 94
- investment in, 85
- rent-seeking in, 59
- state-owned enterprises (SOEs), 82

Small businesses. *See* Enterprise restructuring
Social factors influencing transition, 48–49
Social insurance, 108–109
Socialism, defining, 99
Socialist governments, 57
Socially-owned enterprises. *See* State-owned enterprises
Social safety net
- in Central European countries, 80, 81–82, 87–88
- in China, 48
- under communism, 15, 16
- defined, 112n1
- educational systems, 25, 47, 87
- effects of legacy, 18
- health care systems, 81–82, 101, 103, 104–113
- housing, 17, 19, 20
- pensions, 22, 24, 81–82, 88, 101, 107
- in Poland, 40
- reforms needed, 17, 20, 21–22, 24–25

Social security system (U.S.A.), 100, 112n1
Social unrest in China, 76
Social values and transition, 18
SOEs. *See* State-owned enterprises
Soft budget constraints, 18, 37, 111

Solidarity, moral obligation of, 102–103, 112
Sovereign debt
  Central European countries, 80, 83
  China, 70, 79
  ratings of, 78, 98
  Russia, 60, 61
Specific egalitarianism, 103, 109
Stabilization
  approaches to, 21
  Central European countries, 80, 81
  China, 74
  as criterion for end of transition, 14, 19, 27
  expectations about, 20
  as stage in transition, 6
  planning mentality and, 17
Stabilization-cum-liberalization, 27n4
Standard & Poor's ratings of countries, 78, 98
State
  financing of health care, 105–110
  intervention in life of individual, 102
  regulations and income inequalities, 56
  relation with civil society, 25
  role in market economy, 24, 47
  role in transition, 40
  structural transformation of, 21–22
  weakness of postcommunist, 57–58
State foreign trade organizations, 20
State-owned enterprises (SOEs)
  banks, 70–71, 73
  in Central European countries, 80, 81, 82
  in China, 70, 75–76
  farms, 40, 43
  hospitals in Hungary, 111
  income inequality and, 55–56
  investment demands, 43
  privatization of, 17
  subsidies to, 45, 80, 81
State ownership, of means of production, 17
State procurement, 37
State retail outlets, 20
Stock markets, 21, 38, 67n5, 74, 87
Strategic planning, 17
Street trade, 20
Structural change criteria, 8–9
Structural data for transition countries, 36–38
Structural reforms, 6, 21
Structural transformation
  as criterion for end of transition, 14, 19
  day-one measures for, 20
  mid 1990s, 44
  planning mentality and, 17
  slow pace of, 22–23
Subsidies
  as criterion for end of transition, 77
  to enterprises, 45, 80, 81
  import, 53, 56
  interest, 62
  rent-seeking and, 51
  sources of, 46
Subsidized credits, 53–56, 62, 63
Sustainable growth, 14, 23
Sweden, 100
Switzerland, 40
Systemic criteria, 8, 9
Systemic legacies, 16–17

Tajikistan, 62, 64
Tariffs, 20
Taxes
  as barriers to investment, 86
  distorted structure of, 47
  health care, 108–110
  lowering, 88
  raising, 75–76
  redistributive, 108–109
  shrinking revenues from, 65, 71
  stabilization and, 21
  tax reform, 20
  using to recapitalize banks, 72
Telecommunications network legacy, 18
Trade
  as cause of income inequalities, 60
  See also International trade
Trade balance data, 34–35

Trade liberalization
  barriers to, 61
  in Central European countries, 80, 81
  in China, 69
  in CIS countries, 62
  need for, 20, 77
Trade monopolies in Russia, 60, 61
Trade unions, 25, 58
Transformation, 99
Transition
  barriers to, 23
  in China, 69–76, 79
  countries where completed, 14, 100
  criteria for evaluating, 7–10, 14, 26–27, 39, 77, 99–100
  de-monopolization issue and, 17
  future agenda for, 47–49
  measuring outcomes, 22–23
  models of, 19, 78–80
  outcomes of, 8, 22–23, 39–40, 44–46
  pace of, 10, 40, 41, 49
  social factors influencing, 48–49
  stages of, 6
  vs. transformation, 99
  "when is it over?" 7–10, 27, 39, 65–66, 71–72, 77, 99–100
  See also Economic reform
Transition countries
  compared with developing countries, 26
  data on, 30–38, 93–98
  differences among, 39, 43, 51, 80, 82–84
  geographic groupings of, 15–16
  nation/patient simile, 13–14
  new market economies, 23–27
  See also Asian countries in transition; Central and Eastern Europe; Former Soviet Union
Transition package, 19–22
Transparency, 6–7, 55, 103–104, 108
Turkmenistan
  economic and social data, 31, 33, 35, 37
  lack of economic corrections, 62, 64
  net revenues from credit issue, 54
  rent-seeking in, 60

Ukraine
  central planning, 77
  economic and social data, 30, 33, 34, 36, 93–97
  economic progress (1996–1997), 79
  exchange rate unification, 63
  export and import rents, 53, 62
  income inequalities in, 56
  model of transition, 78–79
  net revenues from credit issue, 54
  reforms, 64
  rent-seeking in, 59
Underground economy, 24
UNDP. *See* United National Development Program
Unemployment
  in Central European countries, 78, 82–83, 87–88, 95
  in China, 79, 90n3, 95
  under communism, 16
  in Czech Republic, 25, 95
  necessary increase in, 76
  rates of, 22, 32–34
  in selected transition countries, 95
  in Vietnam, 79
Unemployment benefits, 81
Unions, 25
United National Development Program (UNDP), 22, 30–31
United States
  health care, 107–108, 111
  social security program, 100, 112n1
  welfare programs, 101
Universal entitlements, 104
Utility prices, 20
Uzbekistan
  economic and social data, 31, 33, 35, 37
  planned economy of, 43

Value, perceptions of, 61

Vietnam
- differences from other transition countries, 6
- economic indicators, 93–97
- geopolitical grouping of, 15
- levels of investment, 83
- model of transition, 79
- pace of liberalization, 43
- pattern of growth, 44–45
- reforms in, 40–41
- state-owned enterprises (SOEs), 82

Visegrad countries, 15, 59
Voucher system
- Czech Republic, 21, 40, 49, 83
- Russia, 55

Wages
- average wage replacement rate, 88
- effect of weakening controls on, 43
- policies, 21
- in selected transition countries, 32–33

Washington consensus, 19
Wealth. *See* Income
Welfare benefits, 81–82, 101
Welfare program, definitions, 101
Welfare reform, 99
Welfare state activities, 101
Wholesale organizations, 20
Wholesale trading in former Soviet Union, 60
Workers
- effects of reforms on, 44
- legacy attitudes of, 18, 19

Workers' councils, 58
World Bank, 2, 27n3
World Development Report (World Bank), 2, 23, 24, 39, 49, 73
World trade. *See* International trade
World Trade Organization, 75

Yugoslavia, 16

Zaire, 40

About the Institute

The W.E. Upjohn Institute for Employment Research is a nonprofit research organization devoted to finding and promoting solutions to employment-related problems at the national, state, and local levels. It is an activity of the W.E. Upjohn Unemployment Trustee Corporation, which was established in 1932 to administer a fund set aside by the late Dr. W.E. Upjohn, founder of The Upjohn Company, to seek ways to counteract the loss of employment income during economic downturns.

The Institute is funded largely by income from the W.E. Upjohn Unemployment Trust, supplemented by outside grants, contracts, and sales of publications. Activities of the Institute comprise the following elements: 1) a research program conducted by a resident staff of professional social scientists; 2) a competitive grant program, which expands and complements the internal research program by providing financial support to researchers outside the Institute; 3) a publications program, which provides the major vehicle for disseminating the research of staff and grantees, as well as other selected works in the field; and 4) an Employment Management Services division, which manages most of the publicly funded employment and training programs in the local area.

The broad objectives of the Institute's research, grant, and publication programs are to 1) promote scholarship and experimentation on issues of public and private employment and unemployment policy, and 2) make knowledge and scholarship relevant and useful to policymakers in their pursuit of solutions to employment and unemployment problems. Current areas of concentration for these programs include causes, consequences, and measures to alleviate unemployment; social insurance and income maintenance programs; compensation; workforce quality; work arrangements; family labor issues; labor-management relations; and regional economic development and local labor markets.